SPENNYMOOR REMEMBEREI

SPENNYMOOR REMEMBERED
BOOK 2

SPENNYMOOR REMEMBERED – BOOK 2

Presentation at the Rink c. 1950.

Among others:
The Band – Charley Stott, Daker Long, Bill Ovington and Carl Gray.
Ned Waterworth, manager, Dave Emmerson, Flo Emmerson, Miss Ross and Harry Lightfoot.

The Rink

The Rink was originally built as a steam laundry, The Lily Laundry. This was followed by Smith's 12 table Billiard Hall. After the 1926 fire at the Co-op premises in Whitworth Terrace, it was used as their warehouse. When the Co-op left it became a roller skating rink, hence the name "Rink," which stuck from that time. During the Second World War the military authorities commandeered the hall to house troops returning from Dunkirk. It was later returned to Hindmarsh Enterprises and resumed use as a Dance Hall under the name Clarence Ballroom. For the last few years of its life it was the Variety Club and many famous bands and artists played there. It was burned down on Tuesday 10th February 1977. Part of Clarence Court was built on the site.

SPENNYMOOR REMEMBERED
BOOK 2

Compiled by
Bob Abley

ARB PUBLICATIONS

SPENNYMOOR REMEMBERED – BOOK 2

First Published 2000
Copyright c. Bob Abley, 2000.

Published by
ARB Publications
98, Durham Road
Spennymoor
Co. Durham
DL16 6SQ

ISBN 0 9536315 1 6

Printed in Great Britain
By
Macdonald Press
Spennymoor
Co. Durham.

SPENNYMOOR REMEMBERED – BOOK 2

Contents

Acknowledgements		6
Introduction		7
1.	In and Around The Town	9
2.	Schools	23
3.	People and Events	41
4.	Trade Transport and Industry	83
5.	Catherine Street and Surrounding Area	101
6.	The Settlement	115

I'm sure that Alan Stoddard and Doug Hindshaw will forgive me if I say that it is the background of the photo that is the most interesting.
The Dicey's School c. 1950.

Acknowledgements

The author appreciates the valuable help given by many people in the preparation of this book. I am more than grateful for the time, information and material freely given. I would particularly like to thank the following people without whose help and encouragement the book could not have been completed: Bill Kitching, Vera Brydon, Milly Carfoot, Tom and Shirley Showler, Sylvia Foster, Edith Kirtley, Lesley and Alister Franks, Mr. and Mrs. Goulder, Bob Jewitt, George and Ella Bulmer, Alf Littlewood, Auralee Gibson, Marie Irving, Enid Barr, Mr. Brownsword, Maureen Ross, Teresa Turnbull, Hazel Whitehead, Jimmy Rooney, Peter Joyce, Mary O'Hara, Joe Prest, Ida and Alec Downham, the Headteacher of North Road School and all at D & A Clemments.

SPENNYMOOR REMEMBERED – BOOK 2

Introduction

The format of this book remains virtually unchanged from the last one, containing photographs and personal reminiscences of Spennymoor and Spennymoor people over the time span of a hundred or so years. Compiling the book has proved to be a constant source of pleasure. Apart from meeting people I have had the added enjoyment of being shown and allowed to copy treasured family photographs, and being regaled with delightful stories of Spennymoor life. Quite a few of the people I have talked to have thought that they had very little to contribute or give, however, once we had a conversation underway what looked on the surface to be a tentative few minutes chat turned into an absorbing couple of hours of education for me. Despite its short history Spennymoor is definitely not short on characters and interesting events. All in all it is the everyday, mundane, life as it is lived events that provide the interest for me, as there is no better way of experiencing what life was like in the town in past generations.

The most significant event affecting the town over the last year has been the closure of Rothmans; Spennymoor is no stranger to blows of this type. However, history tells us that the town and people have the character not only to withstand such a blow but to take it in their stride and to move on to better things.

On the lighter side we have lost a sculpture and gained fountain, one white elephant in exchange for another perhaps?

The shopping centre is still conspicuous by the number of empty shops and its derelict, untidy state at its eastern end. All is not doom and gloom in this direction though; I understand that various initiatives are underway to relieve the situation. Sedgefield Borough Council in co-operation with the Town Council and the Trades Council in the town are taking active steps to improve things. The Borough Council has had a study completed to pinpoint areas of the town that need attention and not only have they formulated a plan of action they have already put it into operation! The Town is to have a Manager, albeit shared with other towns in the Borough. The new owners of the Shopping Centre are making every effort to fill the empty shops and apparently several businesses have shown a serious interest. It has also been agreed in principal that whole of Spennymoor High Street will be opened up to traffic again. The new system will probably be a one way system and hopefully when it is implemented it will help to revitalise the town centre. There is a cautionary footnote though; it has been stated that it may take *several years* to implement the new traffic plan. It will be interesting to see whether all of these proposed improvements will take shape or whether it is all just hot air. Time will tell!

SPENNYMOOR REMEMBERED – BOOK 2

A slight mishap under the bridge.

Motor Bike accident in Low Grange Road

ONE

IN AND AROUND TOWN

Clyde Terrace c.1922.

Known as Carlton Terrace then. The photograph shows the elegant style of the properties at either side of the entrance to Osborne Road, with their elaborate wrought iron decorative work. Note the large greenhouse on the flat roof and the co-op butcher's horse and cart waiting patiently outside the Co-op for its driver. Also the old fashioned telephone pole with the ceramic "dicky birds" sitting on the crosspieces.

Whitworth Terrace c.1922.

Known as Beaumont Terrace in those days. A peaceful scene, traffic free, showing the width of the graceful main road with the bright early morning sunshine showing the frontage of the buildings to their best advantage.

Clyde Terrace c.1922.

Note Doberman's shop on the left, these were Dobermans first premises in the town.

SPENNYMOOR REMEMBERED – BOOK 2

Cheapside c.1922.
A sunny morning. The shops from left to right are Howard Pearson, Whites, Claughan's, Boots, Coia's, Thomas Philips, Commercial Hotel and the Home and Colonial Stores. Note the pawnbroker's sign outside Philips shop.

Cheapside c.1922.
The Arcadia Cinema with Sandersons sweet shop on the left with the Billiard hall above behind the cigarette adverts.

Spennymoor Covered Market c.1910.

This was sited on the High Street in the space occupied by the present Town Hall. The entrance to the hall was under the clock tower, which incidentally never held a clock.

Old Council Rooms.

This was in Silver Street at the back of the Market Hall. These buildings had originally been miners cottages and were purchased from the Shafto Family and converted into Council Rooms to accommodate the Local Health Board, which was established in 1863.

SPENNYMOOR REMEMBERED – BOOK 2

High Street c.1925.
Robert Clough the outfitter, Solomon Doberman's furniture Dealer, Reavley's newsagent and stationer and Hepworths the Tailor are the four shops in the foreground.

Market Buildings, High Street c.1925.
From right to left: Lipton's the grocer, West's the milliner, Hornsby the jeweller, Snowball the printer, The Public Benefit Boot Co., Thompson the drapers and Harrison the bakers.

SPENNYMOOR REMEMBERED – BOOK 2

Ox Close Farm from a watercolour by Robert J. Heslop, painted in 1933.

It is difficult to visualise today but the farm stood on the present site of Ox Close School. This view is from the north, beyond the farmhouse was Spennymoor and the Park.

Ox Close Farm.

My Dad bought the farm in 1939 from Johnny Orton who became the butcher in Merrington Lane. I was just leaving school that year and that's how I became a farmer, I left school at 14 and went straight onto the farm. I didn't know anything about the job but had a good tutor in Bobby Orton who stopped on to work at the farm. He was a good countryman and knew all the ins and outs of the business.

All the work was done by horses in those days. There was a 110 acres of land and much of it was used to graze our cows and the horses, there wasn't as much arable land as there is today. We had 14 cows and four pairs of horses and two ploughs. I had a milk round, which took in all the streets behind the main street, from King Street to the Bridge, I also used to go round the 'blocks'. We got up at 6 o'clock to milk the cows and I was out doing the round with the horse and cart by 9 o'clock. I would spend about two and a half-hours going from door to door with the two and a half gallon cans of milk. The milk wasn't delivered in bottles it was measured out into jugs.

Bobby Orton and myself worked the farm and we hired in casual help when we needed it. Bobby was paid between 30/- and 35/- a week with three half crowns extra for coming in early to feed the horses. In modern money that all comes to the grand total of approximately £2 . 12p.

One of the rooms in the farmhouse was supposed to be haunted. When my brother David was about four or five years old he was put into the room to sleep and the following morning when he got up he said he didn't want to sleep in that room again. When asked why he said that a lady in a long blue dress came and sat on the end of his bed. None of the family slept in that room again after that. The room always felt cold. A few years later we had a guest at the house and he slept in the room for about ten nights. Nothing was mentioned to him about the lady but when he was about to leave he mentioned to my mother that a lady dressed in a long blue dress with a white collar came and sat on the end of the bed. We never did find out who this lady might have been. The house was later converted into two houses and my mother had a grand piano and at times it used to play itself, not a tune but as if someone had run their hand along the keyboard. We never found the answer to this occurrence either.

Mrs. Jewitt with grandson David in front of the Farmhouse c. 1960

We farmed at Ox Close until 1963 when the land was sold to Yuill the builders who built the housing estate shortly afterwards. We then moved to Burton Beck Farm.
Bobby Jewitt

Foundry or Cross Street Merrington Lane c.1957

Tommy White's shop on the right, Mrs. Robsons fish shop in the background and the Dog Track behind that.

SPENNYMOOR REMEMBERED – BOOK 2

The lower end of Coulson Street c.1960.

The photograph was probably taken on a Monday as the washing lines are out in the back streets. The only two buildings which remain today are the Ironworks pub and Brooklyn Garage.

In the left foreground is Brooklyn Garage which was owned by Ernie Brooks of Gyro–copter fame. This building had originally been a crisp factory, built and owned by Keith Kerwood. The original Kerwood crisp factory had been at the rear of Durham Road just off Wood Lane. The new factory didn't last for long as it had to close because of the smell caused by the cooking oil. To the right of the foreground is Cadman's bus garage and a scattering of private garages either owned or rented by local people. The wall running along the road is part of the original wall of the Iron Works, part of it still remains today, the only remaining evidence of the "Works."

The shops from left to right are Waistells the butchers, Joe Goundry, general dealers, Polly Scurr , drapery and Bill Partington general dealers.

The petrol station belonged to Ernie Brooks. To the right of the petrol station is Coulson's Foundry most of it derelict by this time.This was not the original site of the foundry, the original "Dry Bread Works" had been built over the railway line behind Burnett Street in Merrington Lane. They were called the dry bread works because more often than not the men were laid off work due to recession in the industry.

The streets on view are Hume Street and Chapel Street. At one time there was a Chapel at the end of Chapel street but all that remains of it is the plot of land that it used to occupy. The railway line running behind the houses and the foundry was the Ferryhill Bishop Auckland line which separated Low Spennymoor from Merrington Lane.

Half Moon c.1960

Not very much changed today apart from the road system. Who would have thought that back street between Half moon Lane and Salvin Street would become the main road?

Half Moon Lane c.1960

SPENNYMOOR REMEMBERED – BOOK 2

Welsh's Farm Green Lane c.1962.

The Welsh family have farmed on this land since the beginning of the 20th century. Mr. Welsh, father of the present owners, came to the farm from Hett when he was only three weeks old. At the top right of the photograph shows are newly built No. 4 Area Coal Board Offices, later to become the Sedgefield Borough Council offices. It was built on Coulsons Field land not owned by the farm but rented by it. The field had been owned by Coulson's who had the Iron Foundry in Merrington Lane, that's how it got its name.

Coulson's Field was a meadow used for grazing cows, local children used to play in the field I can remember playing cricket, football and flying model aeroplanes in the field during the late 1940's and early 1950's. At the top of the field, near the road , was a large,circular, pot trough that the cows used to drink out of at one time, we all used to sit round the rim with our feet in it. Fortunately there was no water in it at the time.

At this time the farm consisted of about 101 acres extending down from Green Lane to the railway line. Over recent years it has undergone several changes, most of its land being separated from the farm buildings by the Spennymoor by- pass. The acreage has also increased taking in the land once farmed by the Skibereen and Redhall farms.

Most of the houses in Green Lane were large, detached and were occupied by local dignitaries and businessmen.

Whitworth Park

This was the scene at the rear of Whitworth Hall prior to the opencast operations, which took place during the early 1960's.

The same scene during opencast operations.

Sir Lindsay Parkinson Ltd carried out the opencast operations. The diggers they used were so large that they had to be put together on the site and later dismantled when the work was finished. They were also powered by electricity and the Electricity Board had to put in a sub station to make sure they had an adequate supply.

High Street in Sunshine 1954.

High Street under Snow 1954

Aged Miners Homes Middlestone Moor 1912.

The inhabitants lined up for the camera along with the matron in charge. Most of these men would probably be from the Spennymoor area but some may have been from further afield. The various miner's union lodges throughout the County would apply to place members in the homes so some of these men could have come from Crook or Trimdon or from any other mining community in the County.

SPENNYMOOR REMEMBERED – BOOK 2

Gala Day Parade c.1956

The War Memorial and the Central Methodist Chapel 1954.

The chapel the largest in Spennymoor was built in 1855 to accommodate a congregation of 900. It was demolished in the 1960's along with the rest of Bishops Close Street.

I can remember attending a Christmas Carol Service for the combined Schools of Spennymoor conducted by Mr. Roberts in the chapel.

The road in front of the chapel used to be the terminus for the United No's 15(Darlington), 3(Ferryhill), 2(Bishop Auckland via Chilton), Altons later to become TMS (Ferryhill Station) and Jewitts (Page Bank).

TWO

SCHOOLS

North Road School

In 1876 Tudhoe and District School Board was formed with 13 members comprising, Ferryhill, Merrington, Merrington Lane, Low Spennymoor, Tudhoe, Whitworth and Whitworth Without. Sam Adams of Bishop Auckland was Clerk to the Board; F. J. Rowland, N.E. Bank, treasurer, George Peacock, Clyde Terrace and William Blenkin, King Street, Spennymoor, attendance officers. One of the first schools built by the Board was Tudhoe Grange School in Mount Pleasant, it was built and opened in 1879. This School later became known as North Road School. The following is an entry made in Whellan's Directory of County Durham in 1894:

Tudhoe Grange School. A large building in stone, for boys, girls and infants built in 1879 at a cost of about £4,600. In the boys department room is provided for 250 and the average attendance is 150; in the girls, for 200 attendance 140; in the infants200, and attendance 160. The school consists of one large room, two classrooms, apartment for caretaker and a board meeting room.

SPENNYMOOR REMEMBERED - BOOK 2

Boys Department 1879.

The Schools were opened on 3rd November 1879 by the Reverend C. Friskin and W. Johnson members of the Tudhoe and District School Board. Anthony Charlton was the Certificated Teacher in charge of the Schools. During the first week Charlton noted in the school log that the boys were " very dull and very backward in their work". Shortly after opening two pupil teachers, George Hodgson and Thomas Naylor were employed and an Assistant Master, George Peacock to cope with the growing number of admissions.

During the first year 356 boys were enrolled of which 156 left leaving a total of 200 boys on the roll. The average weekly attendance for the year was 150. Absenteeism among both staff and pupils was high. Charlton had cause to complain on one occasion that one of the pupil teachers had been absent 8 weeks since he was engaged. As far as pupils were concerned the excuses were illness, the weather and just obstinate reluctance to attend school.

Charlton also complained about the two pupil teachers not preparing their lessons properly and made particular reference to the lack of discipline in one class on several occasions. George Peacock was regarded as a diligent and hard working teacher.

The school was inspected by Her Majesties Inspector Arthur Bernays on January 2nd 1881 a little over a year after it had opened.

No. Present	Passed Reading	Passed Writing	Passed Arithmetic
118	117	115	112

The overall percentage pass rate was 97.2%

The Inspectors Report.

" I am very much pleased with the results of the examinations which are in every respect highly creditable. T. Naylor and G. Hodgson passed fairly but T Naylor should attend to Arithmetic".

       Arthur Bernays.

Girls Department 1879.

The Headmistress, Helen Scott, had the same misgivings as the Head of the Boys Department as her opening remark in the log book shows, "I find the children very backward in their work".... "Their spelling is defective, they know very little or nothing about grammar and seem to have no understanding even of the most simple parts of speech."

As the numbers grew a pupil teacher was appointed by the Board in December and immediately impressed with her willingness to learn, however her knowledge of grammar was weak. Improvement began to be made in the basic subjects but the Headmistress remarked that the girls were very backward in needlework and were not easily interested in geography.

SPENNYMOOR REMEMBERED - BOOK 2

Absenteeism was a problem, the girls seemed to succumb regularly to Fridayitis. If the weather was bad the girls stayed away in large numbers and there was an epidemic of measles and an epidemic of fever in the district in the first year of it opening.

By April of 1880 the growing numbers merited the appointment of a Certificated Assistant Mistress by the Board. Right from the start the headmistress was not satisfied with her work… "Discipline in the class is very loose" …. "there is no method in her work". In the October a monitor was appointed, she was transferred into the girls department from the infants department. Towards the end of October things came to a head between the headmistress and the Assistant Teacher:

" I have pointed out to Miss …………. some of the reasons for her discrepancy and have shown her how to remedy it".
The next entry in the school log was:
" Miss …………. absent this afternoon through a hysterical fit".

At the end of the first year 317 girls had been admitted and 137 had left leaving 180 on the roll, the average weekly attendance during the year was 128. The girls were divided into standards 1 to 6. The rest of the staff looked after standards one to three while the headmistress took responsibility for standards 4 to 6 herself.

The school was inspected on 21st. January 1881 by the same H.M.I. who had inspected the Boys School.

Number present	Passed Reading	Passed Writing	Passed Arithmetic
101	100	98	98

The overall percentage pass rate was 97.6% slightly better than the boys.

The Inspectors Report.
The Girls have passed a very good examination in the elementary subjects and did extremely well in grammar. I can also report favourable needlework but there is room for improvement in that of the second stage and both gathering and buttonholing need more attention.

So despite misgivings and worries about the capabilities of both pupils and staff I think it might be said that both departments had a successful first year.

Extracts from Log Books.

August 6th. 1880 (Girls)
School reopened on Monday. Find the children very backward after the holidays. The average attendance for the week is 124 being brought down through a severe storm yesterday.

Dec. 10th. 1880 (Boys)
I find that the boys in standard 4 are getting very careless and indifferent with their work, many are failing through carelessness and want of attention.

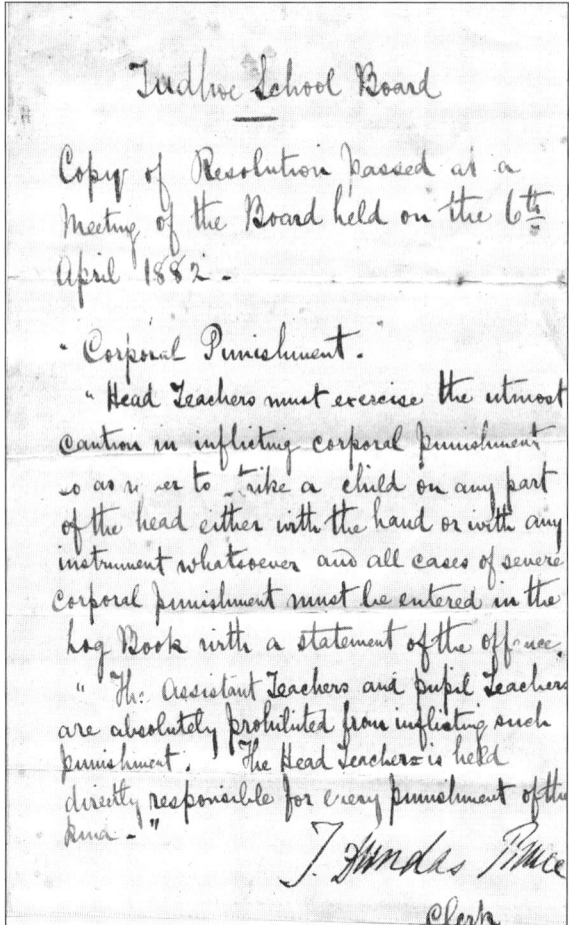

Letter to Anthony Charlton from the Clerk of the Tudhoe School Board Regarding Corporal Punishment in 1882.

Corporal punishment was freely dispensed at this time and physically 'laid on' to maximise the effect. However, it seems, there were limits and one wonders what event or events brought this letter from the Local Board. Whether the warning was just for that school or a general warning to all schools with the control of the Board.

Extracts from Log Books

16th. April 1880 (Girls)
   Average attendance very low this week 109 through sickness.

27th February 1881 (Girls)
   Find spelling throughout the school to be very weak and progress in it only slow.

25th June 1880 (Boys)
   Reading in standard 3 is again acquiring that monotonous tone which was so common at first. I cannot get the teachers to do this work thoroughly well.

Tudhoe (U.D.) School Board.

EVENING CLASSES

Under the above Board, will be commenced on

Monday, Oct. 12th, 1903

AT THE

MOUNT PLEASANT BOARD SCHOOL,

And will be continued throughout the Winter Months, on

MONDAY, TUESDAY, and THURSDAY, in each Week,

Hours—6-30 p.m. to 8-40 p.m.

SUBJECTS:—

Algebra, Mensuration, Arithmetic, Geography, Reading & Writing, Needlework & Drawing.

Teachers - Mr A. Charlton & Assistants

A fee of Two Shillings for the Session will be charged, half of which will be returned to all Students who make 70 per cent. of the total attendances.

These Classes are open to all, young and old, of both sexes.

By order of the Board,

SAM. ADAMS,

Sept. 1903. CLERK TO THE BOARD.

J. Snowball, Printer, &c., Silver Street, Spennymoor.

SPENNYMOOR REMEMBERED - BOOK 2

North Road Cookery Class 1947.
Back Row L to R: Marion Linsley, Joyce Edwards, Margaret Goundry, Sadie parsons, Joyce Gough and Miss Kirk.
Middle Row: Joyce Harker, Hazel Rivers, Margaret Curl, Ellen Kipling and Lizzie Lamb.
Front Row: Mary Kay, Mary Jackson, Rita Robson, Elsie Hopper and Sheila Cooper.

North Road Football Team 1947 – 48

Among others
Mr. Ellison, Mr. Foster.
Arthur Grayson, Jack Dennis and Robert Hepple.

SPENNYMOOR REMEMBERED - BOOK 2

North Road Boys, Mr. Maitland's Class.

Back Row: Eric White, Harry Taylor, Bernard Pringle, Bob Abley, Wilf Temperley, Melvyn Rounsley, Peter Dennis, Ron Farlow and Joseph Goundry.

Middle Row: Walter White, Nathan Card, Billy Swift, Billy Relph, Ray Johnson, Alan Treggoning, Dicky Beavis, Ian Carr, Ray Shearer, Les Lindsay and David Rivers.

Front Row: Ron Bowen, Ray Farlow, Barry Davison, Danny Cartlidge, Tommy Cooper, Mr. Maitland, Alan Sanderson, Jimmy Manfren, Derek Meek, Eric Tolson and Malcom Caufield

The photograph was taken in the April of 1951 and we were nearing the end of our stay in Junior 3. This was our scholarship or 11+ plus year. We seemed to be a happy bunch of lads and had an easy if uneventful year under the eye of Mr. Maitland. This was also the year of the Festival of Britain and I remember a trip to the H.M.S.Campaignia, which was moored at Newcastle, to see the Festival of Britain Exhibition.

My memory is pretty hazy but I can remember being an avid reader of the Eagle comic, which had recently arrived on the scene. In school a new and efficient fountain was fixed in the boys porch which proved a godsend during that summer. Other high spots of the school year were a visit to Tudhoe woods for a nature walk with Mr. Ellison and sports day with its famous 10 lap race that only seniors could take party in. Sports days were very competitive as it was based on a house system. We were all divided into teams, you were a Saxon, a Celt, a Norman or a Dane. On sports day all competitors competed for points in an attempt to become overall champion and to boost your house points total. The winning house had the date of the achievement sewn onto a pennon in the house colour. Individual champions were presented with a cup.

The culmination of the school year was the presentation of prizes for good work, which took place in the hall. The hall was very small and on this occasion the whole school was squashed into it, we didn't much care as it was the last day of the school year and we left for our summer holiday with the sound of rousing cheers ringing in our ears.

SPENNYMOOR REMEMBERED - BOOK 2

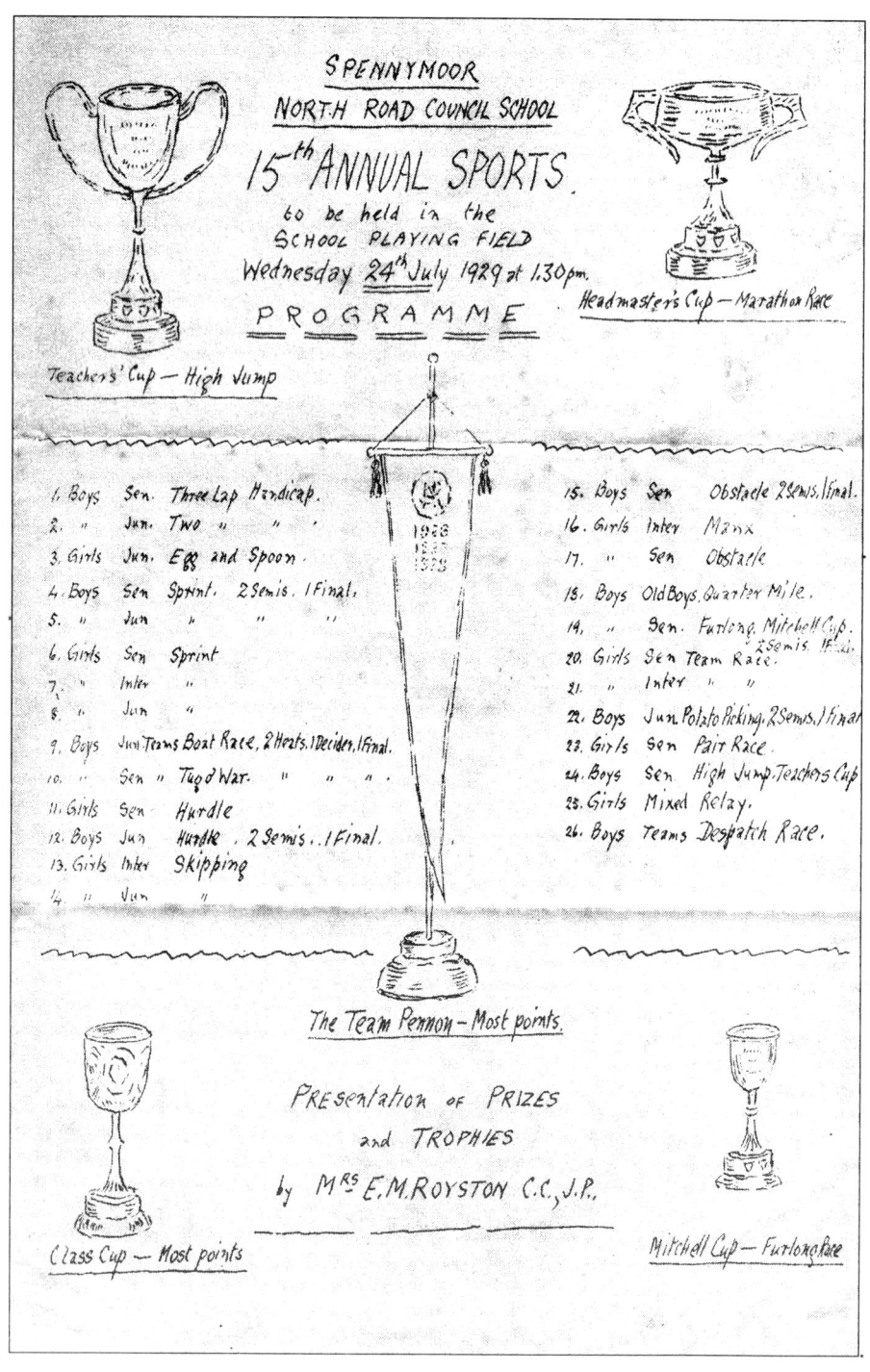

SPENNYMOOR REMEMBERED - BOOK 2

North Road Girls 1950-51.

Back Row: Anne Hopper, Anne Drake, Susan Spowart, Maureen Goundry, Kathleen Robinson, Joan Spence, Nancy Hills, Brenda Lee, Doris Round, Joan Nolan and Margaret Farlow.
Middle Row: June Thornbury, Maureen Corner, Jean Williams, Enid Featherstone, Joyce Lindsay, Anne Nicholson, Audrey Robinson, Joyce Reed, Anne Howells, Betty Heathcote, Anne Heslop and Lydia Garside
Front Row: Linda Barras, Ethel Tolley, Ethel Snowball, Joyce Huthwaite, Miss Rowe, Dorothy Clayton, Vera Pattison, Sylvia Cook, Jean Peters and Jenny Rivers.

I can remember it as a happy and pleasant school where life seemed easy going with very little pressure put on the pupils. We wore blue tunics and green blouses or cardigans, the staff tried to keep us in these as long as possible but when we were in the senior class it was difficult to get tunics to fit. Some of the teachers were strict and from the old school, making sure we were clean and tidy, inspecting our nails and asking if we had cleaned our teeth, one even asking if we had been to church on Sunday and if not why not. We had an assembly every morning and after that it was normal lessons that were basically the 3 R's. We did get other lessons my favourites were History, Art and Cookery. We had cookery with Miss Kirk who was a really nice teacher.

I cannot really remember anyone being really badly behaved but on occasion the cane was used by the Head Mistress Miss Wilson but only for the most serious of crimes. Miss Wilson was a very nice person. We went on school trips to Whitley Bay and greatly enjoyed sports day. There were quite a few girls in our class who were tall for their age and we tended to stick together, walking backwards and forwards to school together and playing together after school. We had parent's days when your Mam and dad came in to look at and discuss your work with the Teachers, I wasn't keen on these days.
    Maureen Goundry

SPENNYMOOR REMEMBERED - BOOK 2

North Road Girls Cookery Class c.1952.

Among Others:
Back Row. Lily Birchall, Ann Jackson, Margaret Bell, Norma Featherstone, Belle Freeman, Olive Williams, Sheila Petch and Betty Richardson.
3rd. Row. Sheila Howe, Joan Spence, Loretta Birbeck, Sylvia Meal and Rosemary Cummins.
2nd. Row. Kathleen Armin, Isabell Green, Margaret Lister, Miss Young, Violet Blood and Joan Meggeson
Front Row. Ann Airey, Mary Wheatley, Gladys Corbet, Ann Brown, Maureen Welsh Doreen Williams.

Extract from a Report from the early 1950's

The girls are daughters of miners, factory and railway workers. A number of them come from a district where there is a good deal of derelict property and several from homes, which are overcrowded. Some families are being transferred to new housing estates. That the pupils, almost without exception, present such a neat, attractive and well cared for appearance reflects great credit on the parents and the girls themselves.

The girls show to advantage in Housecraft; they are competent, reliable and independent. Special interest is taken in the planning, preparing and serving of meals and in the entertainment of guests. Some good needlework, including embroidery, was seen, especially in the lowest class and forms III and IV.

Christmas was the most exciting time at school, there was a carol service held with other schools in the Methodist Chapel in Spennymoor. Each class put on a play and acted them in the week before we broke up also during that week each class had its own Christmas party. Our parents used to provide the ingredients and we used to cook things for the party. I can remember making Christmas Puddings with Miss Kirk and putting silver sixpenses into some of them. Everyone took a present to the party and they were hung on the Christmas tree and at the end everyone got a present. We had a real enjoyable time playing games and dancing.

Maureen Goundry

SPENNYMOOR REMEMBERED - BOOK 2

North Road Girls 1950.
Back Row: Carol Westgarth, Edna Short and Irene Ebden.
Middle Row: Hazel Blood, Margaret Holmes, Margaret Pringle, Margaret Burns, Jean Miller, Rita Foster, Audrey Ivey, Pauline Jackson and Sheila Walton.
Front Row: Mary Ebden, Louise Cunnings, Brenda Bamforth, Agnes Smallman, Barbara Waugh, Mr. Tuck, Marjory Taylor, Margaret Mason, Janet Brown, Joan Savage and Olive Jackson.

North Road Junior School Morris Dancers c. 1960.
Back Row: Timothy Partington, Colin Raw, Alan Lawrence and Christopher Lawrence.
Front Row: Raymond Morgan and John Blench.

SPENNYMOOR REMEMBERED - BOOK 2

North Road Girls Standard 5 c.1951

Back Row:
Irene Dobbin, Hilary Kitching, Alice Brain, Sylvia Dougal, Maureen Bickley, Audrey Thompson, Ann Edwards, Lillian Stoker, Anne Tregonning, Flora Glasper and Anne Dale.
3rd. Row:
Rita Bulmer, Enid Robson, Zena Heathcote, Audrey Scott, Norma Featherstone, Doreen Williams, Margaret Campbell, Mary Stephenson, Beryl Armstrong, Sheila Joyce, Hilda Cornish and Gladys Heathcote.
2nd. Row:
Gladys Corbett, Enid Wright, Pat Lindsay, Maureen Smith, Dorothy Wells, Mavis Blair (teacher), Penelope Brown, Norma Kay, Pam Lindsay, Jean Henderson and Janet Robson.
Front Row:
Marjorie Connor, Vera Brain, Sybil Dale, Anne Joyce, Evelyn Fell and Audrey Ruth.

SPENNYMOOR REMEMBERED - BOOK 2

North Road Boys 1950. Mr. Curry's Class.
Back Row: Raymond Mason, Desmond Patchet, Trevor Harding and Bernard Sanderson.
Middle Row: Norman Harker, Kevin Wayman, John Furnace, Robert Scott, Arthur Meek, Bernard Naylor and Kenneth Todd.
Front Row: James Burdon, William Thompson, Thomas Wetherell, Rene Bee, Mr Currie, Alec Downham, Keith Brown, John Hick and William Target.

North Road Boys, Mr. Pumfords Class 1952
Back Row: Dicky Elgy, Kenny Kipling, Barry Armstrong, John Shearer and Dicky Howells.
Middle Row: Tommy Noddles, Ricky Rivers, Peter Wendell, David savage, Malcolm Knaggs, John Redhead, Brian Henderson, Jimmy White and Gary Lowry.
Front Row: Malcolm Howard, John Parker, Teddy Hedgecombe, Tony Burns, Raymond Petch, Mr. John Pumford, Ray Miller, George Tuck, David Thornbury and Trevor Knowles.

SPENNYMOOR REMEMBERED - BOOK 2

Church of England School Girls c. 1943

The photograph was taken at the school annual camp at Seaham Harbour. All of the girls are from Low Spennymoor some where from Tudhoe School.

Front Row: Una Bott, Doreen Card, Doreen Webber, Janet Lowe, Joan Bainbridge, Catherine Curle and Joyce Clayton.
Middle Row: Doris Spence, Nellie Bartram and Mary Howells.
Back Row: Lily Storey and Vera Farthing.

King Street Girls School Camp at Filey c. 1940.

SPENNYMOOR REMEMBERED - BOOK 2

Upper Church Street School Football Team 1931-32.
Back Row: Mr. Bert Clark, Tommy Irving, Bill Oliphant, Albert Telfer, Tom Machin, Jack Johnson Norman Siddle and Headmaster, Mr. Harold Askew.
Front Row: Jack Edwards, Jackie Knowles, Will Griffith, Ronnie Wallace and John Brain.

Alderman Wraith Girls 1947.
Among others: Pat Lynn, Frances Valks, Ethel Marrin, Marjorie Ouhtwaite, Vera Berriman, Renee Snailham, Audrey Thompson, Nancy Moody, Ida Fishburn, Joan Clark, Audrey Hunter, Enid Lamb, Betty Moon and Margaret Russell.

SPENNYMOOR REMEMBERED - BOOK 2

Rosa Street Nativity Play c. 1962.
Back Row; Marion Skeene, Lynn Philips, Elizabeth Brack, Lynne Armstrong, Ian Hopper and Carol Showler.
Front Row: Barbara Kitson, Steven Taylor, Rita Malloy, Ivan Gardiner, Leslie Stamp and Mandy Walton.

King Street Juniors 1964-65.
Back Row: Mr. Linton, John Sutherland, Peter Atkinson, Peter Todd, Stephen Bainbridge, Tony Wilson, Neville Goulder and Mr. Farrow.
Front Row: Jeffrey Robinson, David Ellis, Allan Cook, Billy Beasley, Gerald Hamilton and Michael Jowett

SPENNYMOOR REMEMBERED - BOOK 2

Alderman Wraith Netball Team 1920-21.

King Street Girls Class 5 1950
Back Row: Barbara Eleanor, Mary Shearer, Elsie Ramshaw, Irene Smallwood, Josie Coulson, Enid Mitchell, Pat Brown, Shirley Wintersgill, Janet Sinclair, Kathleen Walker and Mamie Whitehouse
Third Row: Jean Hood, Ann Ballantine, Eileen Peacock, Margaret Adams, Florence Wilkinson, Joan Lavery, Beryl Littlewood, Dawn Gibson, Margaret Wall, Joy Ashton and Betty Shippen.
Second Row: Doreen Kirkbride, Doreen Suddes, Marion Rutter, Margaret Crooks, Sylvia Newton, Rita Rhodes, Glenys Davies, Gloria Cowan, Pauline Hatton and Miriam Bulmer.
Front: Margaret Patterson, Joan Cornish, Marion Wright and Sheila Marley.

SPENNYMOOR REMEMBERED - BOOK 2

Spennymoor Nursery PTA Christmas Party 1950.

Durham Road Secondary Modern Girls c.1952
Pauline Rennison, Janet Barker, Barbara Ellcote, Brenda Simpson, Leslie Wise, Janet Brayshaw, Betty Fisher, Dorothy Spowart, Freda Kirtley, Aileen Anderson, Betty Foster and Miss Jobling.

THREE

PEOPLE AND EVENTS

Spennymoor Auxiliary Fire Brigade 1960.

Among others:
Don Howells, Peter Kipling, Peter Johnson, David Mothersdale, Ralph Irwin, John Heslop, Laurie McDonald, Enos Jackson, Jim Snaith, Jim Clazey and Peter McGarry.

The Auxiliary Fire Brigade was originally based at the back of the Town Hall. At this point in time (1960) they had moved to a new station in Queen Street in front of the new shopping centre. This station didn't last for very long, it was demolished to make way for the building of the new Lipton's supermarket on the shopping centre and was moved to its present site in St. Andrew's Lane.

SPENNYMOOR REMEMBERED - BOOK 2

The Dees Family 1906.
Back Row: Albert, William, Lottie, John Arthur, Minnie, Tommy and Sally.
Front Row: Lilly, Mrs. Dees, Mr. Dees, Elsie, Florence and Berty

    This handsome family photograph was taken on January 1 in the backyard of 19 Weardale Street where the family lived. The family had moved from Windy Nook near Chester le Street to Spennymoor because Mr. Dees had got a job as a manager in the Iron and Steel Works.

    Two of the brothers became well known North Eastern artists. John Arthur, the eldest brother born in 1875, was perhaps the more talented of the two. He had studied art at the School of Art in Gateshead and had won gold medals as a result of his talents. Despite this he settled for a career in commerce and painted mainly in his spare time. Arthur was 31 when this photograph was taken. He eventually moved back to Gateshead and was active on the Newcastle art scene for many years. He exhibited work at the Royal Academy on two occasions. He died in 1959 and examples of his work can be seen at the Laing Art Gallery in Newcastle and the Shipley Art gallery in Gateshead.

    Herbert Bewick Dees "Berty", born in 1892 and 14 years old when this photograph was taken. Bert studied art when he was young but decided that becoming a painter and decorator was a more secure occupation than being a professional artist. Bert was a member of the Spennymoor Settlement, he helped with the running of the place and also taught painting to the miners. Norman Cornish and John Heslop, both well-known local artists, were numbered among his pupils. He painted many local landscape scenes, some of his watercolours are outstanding, he seemed to have a particular skill in painting trees. Marshall Hall in his Artists of Northumbria 1982 says he also painted many scenes of miner's cottages and miners at work and play in the Spennymoor area. Bert died in 1965. As far as I can gather none of his work is on public view most seems to be privately owned. It would be most rewarding if an exhibition of this artist's work could be arranged in the town.

Saint Paul's Church Lads Brigade 1949.

Among others:
From the back left:
Eddie Airey, Albert Foxton, Vicar Berriman, A. Proud, Derrick Brown.
Front Row:
Ray Taylor, Stewart Skeen, Stan Ross, John Rodmell, Billy Milroy and Alan Bolton.

Vicar Berriman started the Church Lads Brigade when he came to St. Paul's. We used to meet in the Dicey's School Hall once a week and practice our drill. Most of the equipment we had was either donated or borrowed from other brigades in the area. I remember, particularly, that we got a lot of help from members of the Brigade in Crook. Even the uniforms were donated, it was difficult to get a good fit and some of the bigger lads had a struggle to get into their uniforms. This was us bound for the annual camp at Thornton Cleavleys in the Summer of 1949. I had left school and when I came back from camp my Dad had got me a job at Dunelm Granite. Most of the above group were founder members and when we left there was very little interest and the group folded.

Stan Ross

DURHAM COUNTY COUNCIL ELECTION

TUESDAY, MARCH 6th, 1928
Spennymoor Electoral Division.

To the Electors

LADIES and GENTLEMEN,

In offering myself as a Candidate at the forth-coming County Council Election I may say that my knowledge of your district dates back to my boyhood and for the past thirty five years I have been a resident in Spennymoor.

Again since 1925 I have been an Urban District Councillor and a member of the Auckland Board of Guardians. My service on the two bodies named has given me a good insight into the importance of the work of Local Authorities which will be of the greatest service to me should you decide to elect me as your member on the County Council.

The keynote of my policy is economy combined with efficiency in the administration of the affairs of the County. I am thoroughly opposed to waste of Public Money and will if afforded the opportunity, keep a watchful eye on all unnecessary expenditure.

It is of the utmost importance that the crushing burden of the Rates should be lightened at the earliest possible moment.

These high rates are a serious handicap to the industries upon which many depend for their livelihood; they are a source of anxiety to all the various business people in the locality; they are an oppressive burden on the thrifty; and lastly, they are in their ultimate effect a grievous trouble to the ordinary householder tending as they do to an increase in rents.

In fact an easement of this burden would prove a blessing all round.

It is my earnest belief that much can be done by wise administration and wise spending to achieve this desirable object.

To show the effect of the County Council demands on the people in your own Urban Area let me point out that during the present financial year the amount your Local Authority has been asked to provide for County Council administration alone exceeds the amount your Urban Council needs to carry on the work of your own district. This fact alone should stress the importance of endeavouring to get some amelioration.

I cannot promise the electors to do more than outlined above as the immediate and urgent reduction of the Rates is one which should demand the first attention of the newly elected Council.

It is not my intention to hold any public meetings as I hope to be able to make the personal acquaintance, before the day of the poll, of all the electors with whom I have not hitherto come into touch with.

Trusting to be favoured with your vote and support on the day of the poll; I beg to subscribe myself,

Yours at your service,

H. Askew

23, Whitworth Terrace,
Spennymoor.
February 13th, 1928.

Printed and Published by J. Snowball & Son, Park Avenue, Spennymoor.

H. Askew's Election address for the County Council Election of 1928.

King William Street Children celebrating D. Day 1944.

Among others:
Olga Atkinson, Anne Hood, Margaret Herring, Elsie Ramshaw, Jean Hood, Janet Brayshaw, Elsie Atkinson, Margaret Bainbridge, Joyce Bainbridge, Arthur Smith, Sylvia Newton, Mr. & Mrs. Cooper, Dorothy Thompson, Kenneth Parkin, Carol McGough, Eleanor Thompson, Harry Grieves, Gwenda Perry, Steve Ramshaw, John Arthur and Rita Thompson.

The Tivoli Picture House Staff c. 1940.

SPENNYMOOR REMEMBERED - BOOK 2

Spennymoor Telegram Boys 1945.
Back: Alf Littlewood, Front: Henry Thorpe and Eric Hunter.

When I left school in 1945 I went to Raines for an interview for a job, they said they would be in touch. The following day I received a letter, from the Juvenile Employment Exchange, to go for an interview at the Post Office. I had an interview with the Postmaster, Mr. Burden and I started work on the 22nd. August as a telegram boy. That was all I did, deliver telegrams on my pushbike. At this time, just after the war, there was a tremendous increase in telegram traffic. A lot of the business was telegrams from prisoners of war that were being released by the Germans and Japanese and also demobbed soldiers returning from the war. We also delivered maternity telegrams informing relatives of the happy occasion.

We worked three shifts, 8am to 5pm., 9am. to 6pm. and 9 .45am. to 7 . 45pm. The last shift was the worst shift. Fish and chip shop owners usually got telegrams just before they closed informing them of the price of fish. I used to dread the phone ringing after 6 o'clock as I might have to bike up to Merrington to Tot Lumleys fishop or over to Fletcher's fish shop in Post Office Street. The telegrams had to be delivered they couldn't be left until the next day. I worked as a telegram boy up until August 1949 when I was called up to do my National Service.

Alf Littlewood

SPENNYMOOR REMEMBERED - BOOK 2

Hairdressers Conference Spennymoor Town Hall 1948.
Among others: Mr. & Mrs. Christeson, Mr. & Mrs. Woods, Mr. & Mrs. Gibson and Ray the barber who had his shop in Cheapside.

Page Bank Women's Institute Concert 1950.

Tudhoe Colliery Banner being marched into Durham on Big Meeting Day C.1950.

Tudhoe Colliery was opened in 1866 by the Weardale Iron and Steel Company, when most of the coal produced was used by the Iron Works. The pit closed in 1935 but was opened up again towards the end of the war and was known and worked as Tudhoe Park Drift until it closed for good in 1969 some of the workers being taken on at Coutauld's.

The banner, one of several belonging to Tudhoe Colliery over the years, had a picture of the village green on the front and on the reverse side an illustration of the Emancipation of Labour. The banner was acquired by the lodge in 1921 and was paraded at the Big Meeting until at least 1956.

SPENNYMOOR REMEMBERED - BOOK 2

Dean and Chapter Banner outside the Vulcan Pub, Low Spennymoor c. 1950.
Among others:
George Shields, Tommy Wigham, Tommy McGowan, Teddy Shields, Harry Rutherford (landlord), Harry Rutherford, junior, Irene Rutherford and Alderman Billy Hirst

A lot of Low Spennymoor miners worked at Dean and Chapter. The banner is draped in black signifying a recent death in the colliery. Mining was a hazardous occupation and it was a common occurrence for the pit buzzer to sound giving notice that there had been a serious accident or a death in the pit. When the buzzer sounded it struck fear into the wives whose husbands or sons were at work during that particular shift.

" In 1936 during a period of two or three weeks there were five men killed between Dean and Chapter and Mainsforth collieries. All of these men were from the Weardale Street and Bessemer Terrace area."
                    Eddy Goulder

The banner is of interest in that it has the portrait of Billy Todd who was described as follows by Bill Moyes in his Banner Book:
"...A communist agitator who worked actively for better mining conditions Todd was victimised by Durham coal owners and his re-employment in 1941 was said to have been at the intervention of Ernest Bevin while he was Minister of Labour. Within three years of this Todd became secretary of the Dean and Chapter Lodge."

Bill Todd died prematurely in 1946. Dicky Beavis gives this account of the cause of Bill Dodds early demise:
"He was leading a demonstration and he was attacked by police. It was a peaceful march and I've talked with some of the lads who were at the head of the banner. All the

parading police said, "That's him there!" and Billy Todd was struck down. And they say it was from that blow – the repercussions afterwards – that he died in 1946."

The names on the banner are those of Durham M.Ps including Helen Wilkinson M.P for Jarrow. It was a rare honour for a woman to be acknowledged on a banner.

Dean and Chapter Banner c. 1950.

The banner paraded at the bottom of Weardale Street outside the Methodist Chapel, prior to being taken into Durham, on Big Meeting Day. Wherever the starting point for the trip to Durham there was always a good turnout to see the banner off. In the early days they used to walk into Durham with the banner but later took to hiring a bus to make the journey.

"Our lodge banner. I proudly followed it into Durham many times. The portrait is of our late secretary, Bill Todd. When Dean and Chapter closed the Lodge agreed for the banner to be sent to Marx House in London but we had no means of getting it there. As a result, and to my sadness, the banner was lost: it rotted away in the boiler room in the Dean Bank Miners' Institute, Ferryhill."

Dicky Beavis worked at Dean and Chapter off and on from the 1930's until it was closed in January 1966.

Extracts were taken from his Autobiography "What Price Happiness."

Dicky Beavis.

SPENNYMOOR REMEMBERED - BOOK 2

Annie Atkinson at the Bar of the Steam Mill, Merrington Lane c.1960.

Behind the bar with Annie are Mrs. Connor and one of Annie's sisters, Mrs. Jewitt. On the 'right side of the bar' are Daba Foster, Danny Hicks, Chick Snowball, Jack Attley and Teddy Curle.

The Steam Mill must have been built around about the 1860's; it was called the Steam Mill because it was built opposite the steam driven flourmill of Jonathan Parkin. The first recorded landlord I can find is Samuel Piercy in 1879 followed by Patrick Hatser in 1894. Patrick Hatser also had a carters business in Merrington Lane after he came out of the Steam Mill. John Atkinson, Annie's father, appears as landlord in 1902 but he was in the pub before that. John Atkinson died prematurely between 1902 and 1910 and his widow Martha Atkinson took over as landlady and held that position until her death in 1938 when her daughter Annie took the pub on. At that time the pub wasn't doing very well but it took on a new lease of life when the Royal Ordnance Factory opened. Annie who was born in the pub was landlady until she retired in the mid 1960's. She died in 1990 when she was over 90 years old.

SPENNYMOOR REMEMBERED - BOOK 2

Martha Atkinson with her grandson David Jewitt c. 1935.
The photograph was taken in the yard of the Steam Mill in the background is the roof of St. Bede's Church which was a chapel of ease to St. Andrew's in Merrington Lane.

SPENNYMOOR REMEMBERED - BOOK 2

Merrington Lane Ladies, Fancy Dress. Coronation Celebrations 1953.
Back Row left to right:
Ethel Horniman, Lily Taylor, Ethel Blacket, Bessie Goundry, another, Mrs. Connor, Mrs. Williams, Hazel Snowball, Ivy Connor, Mrs. Petch and another.
Front:
Phoebe Porter, Sally Irving, Gracie Johnson, Dora Petch, Annie Kettle, another, and Mrs. Blackley.

1953 Coronation Celebrations Fancy Dress Merrington Lane.
Sally Irving in the pram and Ethel Horniman. Looking along Parkin Street to Coulson's Iron Foundry.

Hearts of Oak Merrington Lane c.1945.

Among others:
Front Row: Mary Richmond, Irene Johnson, Betty White, Sadie Fox, Mrs. Braithwaite, Lily Taylor, Annie Butler and Mrs. Longstaff.
2nd. Row: Mr. Dennis, Mrs. Jemmison, Mrs. Urwin, Mrs. Foster, Mrs. Bella Johnson, Mr. Johnson, Mrs. Tina Porter.
Back Row: Lizzie Curle, Mrs. Dennis, Mrs. Bott, Mrs. Fox, Mr. Homer, Mrs. Robison, Mrs. Grayson and Mr. Dryden.
In Doorway: Ethel Dryden and her Mother.

Parkin Street, Merrington Lane, prior to demolition 1969.

SPENNYMOOR REMEMBERED - BOOK 2

Demolition of Parkin Street March 1970.
The Steam Mill and O'Hara's garage can be seen in the background.

The Snug of the Hearts of Oak c.1950.

Mdlle. Von Etta (La Mystère Indescriptible)

HIPPODROME, SPENNYMOOR,
Monday, February 22nd, and during week.

The Incomparable
VONETTA
in a Startling and Bewildering Act.

Introducing the most gorgeous and costly Scenic and Electrical Effects ever travelled by an Artist.

The staging of this turn alone has cost over £2,000

VONETTA the Acme of Womanly Perfection, and Powerful Company of Vaudeville Stars.

CAMBRIDGE THEATRE, Spennymoor. May 1st, 6 nights
"A MARRIAGE OF VENGEANCE."

MISS A. HARRISON TATE, AS STELLA BURGON

Advertising Postcards for Live Theatre in Spennymoor.

SPENNYMOOR REMEMBERED - BOOK 2

St. Paul's Church on Fire.

On Saturday 25th of July 1953 St. Paul's Church was badly damaged by fire. There had been a wedding at the church that afternoon which finished at about 2.30pm. The vicar and two helpers had remained behind to get the church ready for Sunday, they left at about 3.15pm. At 4pm a lady went into the church to arrange flowers for the next day and noticed smoke and flames coming from the vestry door and raised the alarm. Within the space of a couple of hours the church, apart from the clock tower, was gutted.

A local man, a miner, was later tried and convicted of deliberately setting fire to the church. Apparently he held a grudge because in the previous month he had been convicted in the local magistrates court for stealing the communion wine from the church.

The initial damage was estimated at £10,000 but by the time the reconstruction and repair work had been carried out in 1956 the cost had risen to over £27,000. Almost immediately a restoration fund was set up and efforts to secure grants for the rebuilding were undertaken. £13,525 was received in insurance money, the difference between what was received in insurance money and the actual cost was due to improvements and new building planned by the architect. Donations came from all over including, America, Germany, New Zealand, Australia, Canada, and South Africa. Money was raised by sales of work, gift days, whist drives, plays, concerts and jumble sales etc. The steadiest offerings came from parishioners who subscribed 3d. a week. Saturday coffee mornings raised £900 over three years. The traffic manager of G & B buses used to stop the bus every time he passed the church gates and put a donation in the box.

The architect appointed was Stephen Dykes Bower a leading ecclesiastical architect, he was Surveyor of Fabric of Westminster Abbey and had worked on St. Paul's and Norwich cathedrals. Plans were accepted in December 1954 and work began in May 1955.

SPENNYMOOR REMEMBERED - BOOK 2

St. Paul's as it looked in the winter of 1954.

Interior of St.Paul's before the fire.
Vicar Berriman officiating at the service.

SPENNYMOOR REMEMBERED - BOOK 2

During the time between the fire and the rebuilding of the church normal services were carried on in various places. At first the Church School (Dicey's) was used as the children were on holiday. When the school restarted the Parish hall was used for mid week services and the Sunday services were held in the school. The Harvest Festival and Christmas services were held in the Town Hall in 1953 and from Easter 1954 the Sunday services were held in the Town Hall. Bishop's licenses enabled services to be held in these buildings. Baptisms and Weddings also took place, however burial services were held at either Whitworth or St. Andrew's church. It was a difficult time for all concerned Gordon Berriman, the vicar, and parishioners but despite these difficulties parish life went on with the minimum of fuss.

Vicar Berriman greets the Queen Mother on arrival.

St. Paul's was reopened on November 1st 1956 to coincide with a visit from Queen Elizabeth, the Queen Mother. The reopening and rededication were well publicised and large crowds turned out to see the Queen Mother arrive. I was at Spennymoor Grammar Technical School at the time and the whole school was taken out to line the pavement above the church. The Queen Mother arrived at about 1pm to great excitement and cheers from the crowd.

The rededication of the church was completed the next day, Friday, at a Solemn Eucharist presided over by the Bishop of Jarrow. The first person to be married after the rededication was Doreen Robinson on the Saturday and the first christening took place at 3pm on the Sunday.

SPENNYMOOR REMEMBERED - BOOK 2

The Queen Mother Entering the Church.

The end of the visit.

SPENNYMOOR REMEMBERED - BOOK 2

St. Paul's Parish Dance 1957.
Left to right: Jim Storey, Beatrice Barret, Frank Willis Ron Corker (curate), Doreen Estill, Gordon Berriman (Vicar), Mrs. T.L. Sutton, Betty Berriman, Shirley Sutton and Joe Prest.
This was one of the many dances held by St. Paul's Church members in the Town Hall.

St. Paul's Sunday School Group c.1949.
The Sunday School group were photographed after the Flower Service.
Among others: Deaconess Bridget Smith, Jean Grainger, Anne Wendel, Margaret Shilling and Shirley Sutton.

SPENNYMOOR REMEMBERED - BOOK 2

St. Paul's Church Bazaar 1959.

Among others: Marjorie Stapleton, Beatrice Barret, and Joy Ashton at the St.Pauls' Guides stall.

St. Paul's Church Youth Club Football Team c. 1937.

Among others:
Back Row: Jack Boustead and Bob Lawrence.
Middle Row: Ernie Home, Fred Lightfoot and Ernest Hanselman.
Front Row: Harry Kirk, Ernest Maddison, Bob Stapleton and Norman Ross.

SPENNYMOOR REMEMBERED - BOOK 2

Cambridge Theatre Fire 1972.

The theatre was gutted by fire in the August of 1972. After the fire it was demolished, however, the adjoining Theatre Bar was refurbished, enlarged and reopened as the Pheonix Pub. Eventually it was closed and during recent times was converted into John Willets showroom.

Spennymoor Male Voice Choir c. 1930.
The lady was the conductor of the choir.

SPENNYMOOR REMEMBERED - BOOK 2

Ned Waterworth.

Ned Waterworth.

Ned Waterworth was born in Lancashire in 1903 and moved to Spennymoor when a young boy. He started work at Dean and Chapter Colliery at the age of fourteen and like many young miners at the time he joined the local D.L.I. Territorials. One of the attractions was a fortnights camp which took him and others away from the rigours of coalming. They regarded this camp as their annual holiday. While in the Territorials he developed his prowess as a boxer and he became middleweight boxing champion of the D.L.I. He represented the 50th. Division and became their champion and later he represented the 151st.Brigade in London in 1933 and again won. He retired from boxing in 1935 as undefeated champion.

At the outbreak of the war he was called up into the 6th. Battalion D.L.I. along with his two brothers Hughie and Herbert, all became sergeants. Ned was evacuated from Dunkirk, Hughie was taken prisoner and Herbert was killed on the Belgium border. After the war Hughie became the popular landlord of the Railway Hotel in Spennymoor.

On demob from the army in 1945 Ned became M.C and assistant manager of the Clarence Ballroom, affectionately known locally as the "Rink." In the late 1950's he became Youth Leader at Low Spennymoor Wesleyan Youth Club and as a qualified dance teacher he formed a ballroom dance team which won the Durham County Youth Clubs Ballroom Championships two years running.

He died in Spennymoor in 1992 at the age of 89.

Eddy Goulder

SPENNYMOOR REMEMBERED - BOOK 2

Ned Waterworth in an open-air contest c.1930.
The contest was held at Ripon Camp, Ned is the boxer on the left.

Mount Pleasant Youth Club Gymnastics Team c.1928.
   An interesting photograph taken on the tennis courts behind the Wesleyan Chapel with the Upper Church Street School building to the right and the back of Weardale street to the left.
   Among this group are Ned Waterworth kneeling on the left with Jack Patterson standing in front of him. Jack was a local champion with the Indian Clubs he used to give demonstrations with them.

SPENNYMOOR REMEMBERED - BOOK 2

Mount Pleasant Youth Club Ballroom Dancing Champions c.1955
From left to right: Marion Horn, Ronny Dent, Ned Waterworth, Dorothy Wells, Alan Taylor, Yvonne Carling and Bob Taylor.

Representatives of the Youth Organisations in Spennymoor c. 1955.
Among others Walter Cook, Vera Button, Vicar of Holy Innocents Nancy Stapleton, Arny Stapleton and Ned Waterworth. Mr. McDonagh County Youth Officer.

SPENNYMOOR REMEMBERED - BOOK 2

Royal Ordnance Factory Group c.1940

Among others:
Tommy Mooney, Vera Rose, Beatrice Thrower, Allie Redhead, Mary Carmady, Betty Atkinson, Ethel Lamb, Eva Sokell, Edith Wigham, Betty Carmady, Marion Robinson, Edna Stonehouse and Olive Atkinson.

Royal Ordnance Factory Girls c. 1940.

Among others: Dot Healey, Millie Wigham, Kathy Lamb and Ivy Gibson..

The photograph was taken outside Viners Close cottages by Mr. Laylock the photographer who worked at the factory at that time.

SPENNYMOOR REMEMBERED - BOOK 2

Royal Ordnance Factory 1940.

We worked three shifts at the factory, 6am until 2pm, 2pm until 10pm and 10pm until 6am. The men worked 12 hour shifts, When the factory opened after the outbreak of the war a gang of us, all friends got jobs together. As the factory expanded we all ended up working in different places.

On Fridays when we were on the 2pm till 10pm shift we would bring our best clothes with us to work. When we finished work we would go to Mrs. Griffith's house in Merrington Lane, have a cup of tea and then change out of our work clothes. We would then walk up the black trod to the "Rink" for the 10 'til 2 dance, getting there by 11 o'clock. Everybody went to the "Rink" in those days, lots of girls I knew met and married soldiers at the rink, and then moved away. The soldiers were from Brancepeth Camp. One lad we knew who went to the "Rink" used to bike over from Brandon.

Millie Wigham.

War Savings Group c. 1940

Among others:
Mrs. Pennington, Mrs. Plumb, Margaret Wheatman, Mrs. Hansleman, Bessie Dobson, Mrs. Harbottle, Mr. Marley and Mr. Robinson.
Every effort was made to get people to save to help the war effort and groups like these were set up to do this in towns and villages throughout the country. This group are advertising their effort with the aid of a bomb!

SPENNYMOOR REMEMBERED - BOOK 2

War Effort Scrap Collection c.1940.

Among others: Derek Mapp, Gordon Brooks, Neville Rutherford, Shirley Sutton and Jack Chicken.

This group of collectors operated in the Durham Road area in a scheme organised by Mr. Rutherford from the shop on the corner of Brook Street. We used to collect newspapers, scrap metal, bottles, old car tyres and anything that could be recycled to help the war effort. We were given points for every item that we brought in, the number of points we got depended on the item we had, for example a car tyre carried more points than a bottle. At the end of a collecting period the one with the most points got a half a crown savings certificate as a reward for their efforts. Mr. Reynolds used to store the items on the shelves in the shop, each shelf holding a different category of scrap, it was a regular Alladins cave of junk.

Billy Scorer

I can remember being well in the lead with points to get the halfcrown saving certificate only to be pipped at the post by Shirley Sutton who had managed to scrounge a car tyre from somewhere.

Colin Welsh

SPENNYMOOR REMEMBERED - BOOK 2

Tudhoe St. David's Church Choir Outing 1950.
Among others: Peter Hempson, Brian Hempson, Fred Curry, Billy Briggs, Kenny Gittens, Tony Gittens, Mrs. Gittens, Bob Straugher, Eddy Burton, Vicar Walker, Mrs. Vester, Mrs. Gibson, Tom Vickers and George Gibson.

Holy Innocents Church Choir c.1955
Among others:
Mr. Neasham, Alan Taylor, Derek Lindsay, Don Howells, Tom Ward, Alaister Franks, George Courtney and Mr.Swales.
David Button, Norman Dykes, Peter Slack, John Temperley, Alan Wright and Peter Wendel.
Brian Hudson, Mrs. Swales, Vicar Johnson, Alan Holmes and Michael Hudson.

Tudhoe Parish Youth Club London Relay 1963.

Among others:
Michael Hudson, Cliff Marshall, Alaister Franks, Alan Wright, Chris Camm, John Nichols, David Wilson, Dougy Brass, George White, Billy Gillan, Arthur Saw, Brian Brown, Brian Henderson, Anothny Doyle, Colin Greg, Nancy Stapleton, Brian Lowes, Arnie Stapleton and Bruce Crawford.

The Tudhoe Parish Youth Club undertook the London Relay as a Charity Run to celebrate the 10 years that the Queen had been on the throne. The above crowd are the lads that took part.

The run started on a Friday night and the run was done in three-mile stints. Adams and Gibbons lent the Youth Club two vans and Esso gave them petrol vouchers. The running kit was also provided by sponsors, they had Dunlop White Flash sandshoes and Umbro shorts and shirts in blue. Wrigleys provided them with chewing gum and they had a plentiful supply of mars bars The Milk Marketing Board provided them with ice cold milk.

They completed the run well within their schedule and arrived in London in the early hours of the Saturday morning and consequently found that they had more time to spare than they thought. It was suggested that seeing as though they had completed the downward run so quickly they might run back instead of drive back. This idea was dropped because quite a few of the lads had to be at work on Monday morning.

The first baton change at Chilton.
Arthur Saw passes the baton to Alaister Franks.

Tudhoe Parish Youth Club Members 1962.
Among others: Janet Cook, Margaret Hinton and Nancy Stapleton.
Michael Hudson, Alaister Franks, Arnie Stapleton, Frank Mitchell, Alan Parry and Dave Savage.

SPENNYMOOR REMEMBERED - BOOK 2

Spennymoor Workman's Club Comic Football Match c.1955
The annual Good Friday fancy dress match at the Brewery Field. This is the Spennymoor Club Team: Left to right: Bobby Lowe, Chris Bestford, A. Edwards, C. Bussey, Alf Bateman, T. Bussey, C. Mayhew, Norman Bulmer, J.Elliot and Jobey Martin.

Spennymoor United 1973
Left to right: Billy Robson, Bert Elliot, Jimmy Goundry, Peter Joyce, Kevin Reilly, Neil Walton, John Heavysides, Allan Kell, Butch Simpson, Albert Hickman and Brian Mulligan, David Bradley (mascot) John Davis, Geoff Hart and Kenny Banks.

SPENNYMOOR REMEMBERED - BOOK 2

Spennymoor United end of 1967 – 68 Season.
Players: Albert Hickman, Ray Morgan (mascot), Peter Joyce, Ralph Wright, Graham Defty, John Tobin, Kenny Banks, Eric Hume, Billy Lovejoy and John Wilkinson.

The players and supporters celebrate the end of a very successful season after completing the treble. League Champions, County Cup Winners and Northern League Challenge Cup Winners. Heady days indeed!

Spennymoor United 1963.
Back Row: Jack Flanagan (trainer), A. Iceton, G. Defty, P. Joyce, R. Ellen. A. West. B. Berriman and J. Brown.
Front Row: B. Morris, J. McGeorge, H. Bell (manager), D. Fawell and K. Banks.

SPENNYMOOR REMEMBERED - BOOK 2

Low Spennymoor Methodist Sunday School c.1930
Among others: Back Row: Amelia Jones, Alice Snow and Nellie Machin.
Front Row: Mr. Snow, Ivy Shippen, Robbie Lowe, Albert Richardson, Norman Machin, Doreen Penwick and Tommy Richardson.
This was the chapel in Half Moon Lane.

Half Moon Independent Methodist Chapel c.1950
The installation of the new pipe organ in the chapel. Mr. and Mrs. Pennington, Syd Bakewell, Harry Gibson, Mrs. Wells, the organist and Mrs. Lawrence.

SPENNYMOOR REMEMBERED - BOOK 2

Salvation Army Sunday School Anniversary c. 1955.

Among others: Ian Tolley, Ann Raffel, Ken Johnson, Audrey Johnson, David Piper, Sheila Wigham, Bram Bulmer and Jennifer Piper.

An annual event, the children of the morning and afternoon Sunday Schools were driven round the streets of Spennymoor in Key's coalwaggon under the supervision of Ernie Buston and Les Piper to advertise the anniversary.

Spennymoor Citadel Songsters c.1960.

SPENNYMOOR REMEMBERED - BOOK 2

Carry On Spennymoor, Town Hall c.1949

Among others:
Back Row:
Hazel Spark, Jenny Hall, Mr. Pumford, Greta Parkin, Jackie Dunn, Vera Button, Jean Grainger, Norman Pearson, Joyce Parkin, Gwen Oxenham, Mr. Spark, Ester Cornish, Mr. Harvey, Miss Parkin and Edith Cornish.
Front Row:
Valerie Andrews, Rita Cole, Joan Smith, Hazel Courtney, Joan Lavery, Glenda Gooding, Jean Turnbull, Joan Wigham, Doreen Boyes, Carol McCavanagh, Marie Hall, Lily Brass, Margaret Glaister, Enid Mitchell and Pat Brown.

This was a production put on by the Central Methodist Youth Club. They were very keen on producing shows at this time. Most of the shows were rehearsed and put on in the Central Methodist Schoolrooms in Bishops Close Street but this one with such a large cast was performed at the Town Hall.

I can remember that we rehearsed for this show in the schoolrooms, we used to go two or three times a week. We had to provide two sets of costumes for ourselves. Mine was made by my friend Pat's mother Mrs. Brown, who lived next door to us in Works Cottages. She made the skirts out of old blackout material. Apart from rehearsing for shows we played the usual youth club games such as table tennis etc. There was a continuos series of shows produced by Norman (Tot) Sloane and Mrs. Martin who came from Ferryhill.

Enid Mitchell

SPENNYMOOR REMEMBERED - BOOK 2

Central Methodist Pantomime 1955

Among others:
Mary Bowes, Edith Cornish, Ester Cornish, Yvonne Close, Ernie Henderson, Hazel Spark, Doris Wilkinson, Bob Hesletine and Mr. Bell.

HMS Spennymoor, Central Methodist Hall c. 1950.

Among others:
Back Row: Mr. Lewis, Mr. Vogwill, Cliff Harrison, Tony Adams, Ralph Vogwill, Mr. Harvey and Arthur Pearson.
Front Row: Charlie Button, Mr. Lewis, Mr. Pumford, Mr. Sams, Colin Makeson, Norman Sloane, Fred Dodgson and Mr. Spark.

Smart and Brown Time Office Netball Team 1959-60.

Among others:
Marie Irving, Ann Campbell, May Meggison, Anne Mattimoe, Sylvia Crake, Dorothy Wells and Jean Meggison.
This was a successful season for the girls as the won both the cup and shield.

Women War Workers Tudhoe Colliery Silica Brickworks 1914 –18.
An interesting photograph underlining the important part that women played in all types of industry during the First World War. Only one person is known on the photo. Matilda Eggington, she is in the middle row third from the right.

Remains of the Arcadia Cinema after the fire of 1929.

Pools Win c.1950

Mr. George Barret a 70 years old retired school teacher and vice chairman of Spennymoor Urban District Council receiving a cheque for £14,454 which he had won on the football pools.

SPENNYMOOR REMEMBERED - BOOK 2

Duke of Windsor at Nutters Buildings

Among others: The Duke is about to shake the hand of Mr. Lindsay standing at the yard gate with his wife and daughter Betty. In the next yard are Mrs. Banner and her son Jack. Hetty Dent is the lady at the front of the group in the background.

Weardale Street Children Coronation day Celebrations 1953.
Frank Billingham, Sheila Howe, Eric White, Margaret Bell, Kathleen Summerson, Marion Lowe, Sid Thompson, Marie Billingham, Christine Wigham, Pauline Mason,

SPENNYMOOR REMEMBERED - BOOK 2

Stephen Ross, Lorraine Ross, John Lamb, John Summerson, Alan Wigham, Pauline Lowe, Brian Anderson, Robert Anderson and Colin White.

Weardale Street Men, Coronation Celebrations 1953.
Back Row: B. Evans, S. Bott, F. Billingham, T. Lamb, Mr. Lane, R. Anderson and T. Ellis.
Middle Row: Mr. Robson, G. Kirkbride, B. Bell, Mr. Durkin, J. Harris and J. Lawson.
Front Row: T. Ross, B. Evans, T. Thompson, R. Evans and F. Billingham.

Weardale Street Ladies, Coronation Celebrations 1953.
BackRow: A. Billingham, J. Evans, T. Warren, E. Lowe, J. Ross, Mrs. Evans, Mrs. Lane, J. Ross, S. Dunn and L. Amos.
Middle Row: Mrs. Thorpe, Mrs. Lowe, Mrs. Billingham, Mrs. Dalkin, Mrs. Wigham, F. Wigham and V. Lowe.
Front Row: A. Card, H. Lamb, A. Bell, E. Wigham, M. Jones and Mrs. Thompson.

FOUR

TRADE, TRANSPORT AND INDUSTRY

Brownsword's Chip Van 1931.

Chipvans like the one above are part of the folklore of Spennymoor. Whenever people talk about old times it's not long before chipvans enter into the conversation. This particular van stood outside the Railway Hotel on the main road above the bridge. The traffic was so busy and dangerous even then that it was decided to move it across the road onto the K.J.H. corner in Charles Street. The chip van belonged to Fred Brownsword who is in the van with his young son Fred junior. Raines the coachbuilders built the chipvan and it was painted and decorated by Joe Burgess of Ferryhill who can be seen standing at the right of the van. Joe was a friend of Mr. Brownsword, they had become aquainted shortly after Joe had returned from America. He had been walking down the High Street in a fur coat that he had brought back from America, Fred asked him why he was wearing a fur coat and received the reply that it had been really cold in America. From that meeting they struck up a friendship.

The chip van was kept at the top of Barnfield Road and was transported backwards and forwards by horsepower, there were two horses Prince and Ginger. The ground rent for their pitch outside the K.G.H. was 7shillings and 6pence a week today's equivalent being 35/1/2 pence. All the cooking was done on coke fires and apart from passing trade they used to get a lot of custom from people who went dancing at the Rink. The chipvan stood on this spot until 1939 when the war broke out.

Wedding Day of Fred Brownsword and Edith Williams 1917.

The wedding group consisted mainly of the bride's family, Mr and Mrs. Evan Williams and her two brothers Alfred and William and younger sister Gladys.

Fred Brownsword came from Burslem and came north to work in Spennymoor with Wards of Sheffield. Wards had been contracted to demolish the Iron Works and they employed Fred as a crane driver. Ethel Williams lived with her parents in Barnfield Road and Fred used to wave to her as he was driving his crane on the iron works site opposite. After completing the demolition job Fred stayed in Spennymoor, he then worked for Kenmirs before buying the chipvan. After the war he and Arthur Williams bought an American wagon with a low loader body with six wheels and built a chipvan on it, which was christened "The Roaring Twenties". They used to tour race meetings with it and they charged 4d. for the chips, they only charged 2d. at home in Spennymoor. Eventually Mr. Brownsword became a partner in the Weardale Café in 1942.

SPENNYMOOR REMEMBERED - BOOK 2

Moores Stores c. 1935.

The shop was on the corner of High Street and Duncombe Street and was a well-established and patronised business in the town. The prices in the window are difficult to read but you can just make out Danish Bacon 7d and Danish Butter 1/1d.

I started working at Moores straight from school at 14 years of age. I worked there until I was 18 when I went to the R.O.F. to do war work. I started work usually before 8 o' clock on a morning and on Saturdays had to work through until 12 midnight. Saturday was a really busy day for the High Street, both sides of the street were lined with market stalls and they kept open until late on the night until people stopped coming. There were always lots of people about and the shops stayed open to catch there custom. When the shop did close we had to stop to make sure everything was tidy. There were very few pre-packed goods in those days and we had to weigh everything out from potatoes to sugar, it was hard work. Mr. Carrick was the manager, his daughter also worked there, Eddy Stubbs and a lad called Worthy also worked there. I earned 5 shillings a week (25p) and paid a shilling board to my mother for my keep.

Auralee Gibson

SPENNYMOOR REMEMBERED - BOOK 2

George Bulmer on the Store Butchers Cart in Bishops Close Street c.1959.

Horse transport was still in common use at this time. The Bishop Auckland and Spennymoor Co-op used horse transport for all of its deliveries at this time. The horses were kept in the stables at the back of the Co-op in Whitworth Terrace.

I started on the milk cart in 1956, everything was delivered by horses then. There were 2 bakers horses, two milk horses and horses for the fruit cart. In all there were about 12 horses stabled behind Whitworth Terrace. Tommy Neasham, was the horsekeeper, he was responsible for keeping them in good condition for their work.

Tommy Neasham the Horsekeeper c. 1957

I eventually ended up in the butchery department on the delivery cart, the manager then was Jack Myers. Other people in other departments on delivery were Bill Taylor on the bakery cart, George Lindsay on the fruit cart and Jack Sorley on the grocery cart.

SPENNYMOOR REMEMBERED - BOOK 2

My round for the week used to be: Merrington, Leasingthorne, Merrington Lane, Low Spennymoor, Tudhoe Moor, Tudhoe and Croxdale. Leasingthorne was the really busy part of the round as there was no butchers shop there, I used to take quite a bit of money there.

The cart that I drove had a water tank for washing my hands and to give the horse a drink. If I was caught out on the road in the dark the cart had candle lamps at the front and carbide lamps at the back, all very primitive by todays standards. Riding around on a horse and cart everyday wasn't without incident I can recall a number of occasions when things didn't go according to plan.

One winter day in the early 60's I can remember going to Arthur Stephensons Farm at Leasingthorne, the snow was deep and high and I was unable to turn the cart round to get back to the main road so I had to back the horse out. I was frightening and the horse at times was on its knees between the shafts. I was really thankful to get home that day.

On another occasion I was going down Dean Road, in Low Spennymoor, and the horse which was nervous shied at a manhole cover. At the same time Dr. Hernet was coming the other way in his Ford Consul. The horse took off and in doing so took the side off the doctor's car. Whenever the doctor saw me after that he turned and went the other way.

One afternoon I was down Tudhoe Colliery it was getting dusk and was becoming difficult to see. An empty clothes line had been left strung across the street the horse walked into it and bolted and I ended up being pulled over the back of the cart by the clothes line.

Eventually the horses began to be replaced first by electric vans (Earlybirds) for the milk and then Austin A30 vans for the butchery department I didn't pass my driving test and my horse was the last to go. I went to work for Eastman's the butcher in Cheapside after that.

George Bulmer

View of the cart showing the water tank. The young passenger is Neil Taylor.

SPENNYMOOR REMEMBERED - BOOK 2

Jewitt's Buses.

Grandfather Jewitt came from Hamsterly to Spennymoor in the late 1800's, he came from farming stock. He used to hawk fruit round the streets and sell sawdust to the pubs, they were the days when sawdust used to be scattered on the pub floors. He then bought a coal business and that lasted till the end of the First World War. When my Dad Tommy came home from the war he used his gratuity to buy a bus and that's how they got started with the buses. It was all private hire at first and then it progressed to transporting miners to the outlying pits, Ferryhill, Mainsforth and Bowburn. The first bus they had was a Garford and they began work with it in 1919. When my grandfather was driving he used to be dressed as though he was driving horses even down to the gaiters, he couldn't get away from the horses or his farming background.

They started the run to Page Bank when they coal company stopped transporting the men by tram. The trams were lowered by rope, from a winding house off Carr Lane, down the old Page Bank Branch, to the Page Bank Pit. The bus service proved to be a really busy run and they did really well from it, Page Bank was a busy little place in those days. The bus used to leave Spennymoor on the hour and return from Page bank on the half-hour. Page Bank closed in 1936 because they couldn't cope with the water coming into the pit.

In their heyday Jewitt's employed quiet a lot of people as they were transporting miners to all the outlying pits. Each pit operated three shifts, fore shift, back shift and night shift which all added up to a large number of men who needed transporting. The buses weren't built for comfort, they had wooden slatted seats because the miners travelled in their dirty pit clothes on the journey home, in the days before pithead baths.

The Garford Bus outside the Royal Oak in Church Street c. 1920

A touring party bound for whom knows where. The driver and owner, Tommy Jewitt, is standing on the step of the bus. Among others are Messrs. Brown, Cottrill, Pincher Hunter, Marley, Newton, Warren and Browning. The bus looks as though it has no windows but they could be raised and lowered by leather straps.

SPENNYMOOR REMEMBERED - BOOK 2

Williams Fruit cart 1913

Mr. Williams in the doorway behind the horse and his two sons Wilfred and Arthur. Mr. Williams bought the fruit cart to set his sons up in business after he had lost his two eldest sons in a mining accident at east Howle Colliery, he was determined that he would lose no more sons to the pit. Unfortunately, Wilfred the younger of the two surviving brothers died from pneumonia not long afterwards. Arthur later had a chipvan in Spennymoor outside the Commercial Hotel in Cheapside, eventually he left Spennymoor to live in Northumberland. The photograph was taken at the top end of Barnfield Road.

Phillipson's Shop.

Situated in Durham Road on the corner with Brook Street. Mr. and Mrs. Phillipson had been in business in these premises from the mid 1920's until about 1955. It was a general dealer's shop and sold virtually everything from clothing to groceries.

The window facing Durham Road displayed clothing and the one facing into Brook Street groceries.

SPENNYMOOR REMEMBERED - BOOK 2

Wise's Wet Fish Shop 1950.

George Wise the proprietor is standing in the doorway. He came to Spennymoor from Gateshead to start his business, which he operated until closure in 1968. Wises Fish van was a regular sight in the streets of Spennymoor for several years.

Interior of the shop during the Coronation celebrations of 1953.

SPENNYMOOR REMEMBERED - BOOK 2

View of theFactories in Merrington Lane – Looking North c.1960

View of the Factories in Merrington Lane –Looking South c.1960

SPENNYMOOR REMEMBERED - BOOK 2

Byers Green Old Station.

This was the second station to be built for Byers Green, it was actually sited in Todhills within the bounds of what is now the brickworks. It was built to accommodate a newly inaugurated passenger service in 1878. The platform can be clearly seen as can the engine shed behind the station. The engine shed is still standing.

Byers Green Station c.1960.

This was the third and last station built at Byers Green, it was opened in 1885 to accommodate passengers travelling on the newly built Bishop Auckland Branch.. It closed to passengers in 1939 and to goods traffic in 1958.

SPENNYMOOR REMEMBERED - BOOK 2

Coundon Station c.1950.
The station was opened in 1885 to accommodate passengers on the newly opened Bishop Auckland Branch. Passengers could travel east to Ferryhill or west to Bishop Auckland. It was closed to passenger traffic in 1939 and to goods traffic in 1956.

Croxdale Station c.1948.
This was the nearest mainline station to Spennymoor and perhaps the earliest terminus for buses to and from Spennymoor. It was opened in 1872 and closed to passenger traffic in 1938. It closed to goods traffic the following year. Note the station building on the bridge.

Page Bank Junction c.1950.
This was to the west of the station over the bridge. To the right is the entrance to the goods station with Rosa Street School in the background. To the right is the curve of the line that used to take the branch down to the banks of the River Wear and Page Bank Colliery. This branch closed when Page Bank Colliery closed in 1936.

Spennymoor Station c. 1950.
A good shot showing the full extent of the long platform with the rounded shadow of Dean and Chapter pit heap in the background.

SPENNYMOOR REMEMBERED - BOOK 2

Spennymoor Station c. 1950.
This shot is looking east toward Ferryhill

Spennymoor Station c. 1950.
This view is looking west, note the signal gantry and the station masters house in the background. To the left-hand background is the pyramidal shape of Whitworth Colliery pit heap.

SPENNYMOOR REMEMBERED - BOOK 2

Wilkinson's bus outside Ted's Snack Bar c.1955

The bus is a Leyland Tiger Cub with a Burlingham body it is practically brand new as it came into service in 1955. The registration is TPT 450 and its fleet number 50. Note the cobbles

Wilkinson's bus outside the Vane Arms c. 1964.

This bus came into service in 1959 and is an AC Reliance with a Plaxton body. Registration number 56 DUP and fleet number 56. It is on the Willington run which was started in 1963.

SPENNYMOOR REMEMBERED - BOOK 2

Wilkinson's bus rounding the Bridge Inn Corner. 1963

An AEC Reliance chassis with a Roe service bus body. This vehicle was first registered in 1958. Registration number YPT 470, fleet number 68. Apart from the bus an interesting photograph, Doggart's are having their extension built across the entrance to what was Catherine Street and The Lord Raglan Pub, on the corner of Villiers Street, has been demolished to make way for the entrance to the new shopping centre.

Doreen and Alf Clements.

Doreen Clements started in business in the late 1940's as a hairdresser and around 1954 began selling drapery and fashion goods. After the birth of her son Martin in 1956 her husband Alf joined the business and they worked together from their shop in Merrington Lane. In the early 1960's they opened a grocery shop in Coulson Street and when the Council decided to demolish Merrington Lane the drapery shop was also transferred to the premises on Coulson Street. Both of these shops ceased trading in 1971 when Alf became very ill.

Early in the 1960's they opened a Drapery and fashion shop at 16 King Street, the property had previously been used as a Dentists Surgery. This shop is still open and run by their daughters Patricia and Pauline.

In 1978 Doreen and Alf bought Eric Web's shop on the corner of King Street and Cheapside where with family help they sold Fruit and Veg, confectionery and cigarettes This shop closed with the demise of Bessemer Park flats in 1990.

Doreen Clements Fashion Show, Columba Hall c. 1965.
The models from left to right are: Leslie Beattie, Gladys Smith, Jean Murray, Julie Valente, Pauline Clements, Ann Young, Patricia Clements and Florrie Murray.

The Catwalk Columba Hall c. 1965.

SPENNYMOOR REMEMBERED - BOOK 2

Santi Alonzi

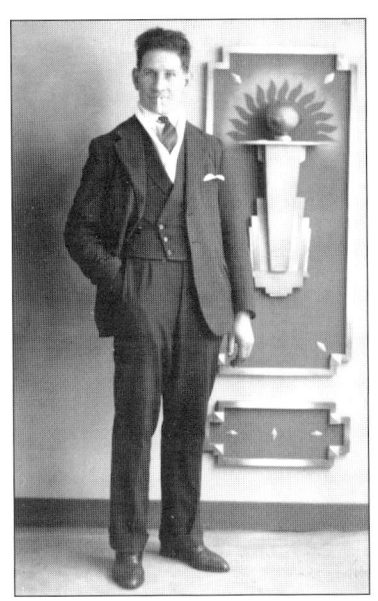

Santi Alonzi c.1923 .

Santi's first wife Regina.

Santi "Sandy" Alonzi was born at Picinisco in Italy in 1997, he came to England in 1923 and settled first of all in Lambeth, London. Later he moved north to live with his sister at 7 Dean Road in Spennymoor. His sister had married a Valente and they ran their ice cream business from the shop in Dean Road. Santi later married Regina "Gina" Valente, so brother and sister married brother and sister. Santi first went into business on his own account in Hartlepool but later moved back to live with his sister in Spennymoor, and eventually bought the shop in Dean Road when his sister and her husband moved to Browney. When Santi and his wife first took over the shop they had a real hard time, Regina even used to chop and sell sticks to make ends meet. Santi became a naturalised British Citizen in 1947. Apart from selling ice cream they also used to sell drapery in the shop during the early days. After the death of Regina Santi married his second wife Anna and they continued to run the shop until it was demolished during the early 1970's.

Santi was a familiar and popular figure around the town with his ice-cream cart and his snack bar was a popular port of call for a lot of youngsters in the Low Spennymoor area. I was a regular customer there every Sunday, along with other members of Holy Innocents Church choir, I used to illicitly spend 3d out of my 6d collection money on sweets to eat in church. On special occasions, i.e. when I was in the money, I used to go and sit at a table in the snack bar and order ice cream and monkeys blood; it was served in a little glass bowl with a wafer stuck in the top. If my memory serves me right this cost 6d. The snack bar was spotlessly clean and Anna who served behind the counter would stand for no nonsense, She couldn't speak English very well but at the first sign of high spirits or rowdy behaviour she would wag her finger at us and that would be enough.

SPENNYMOOR REMEMBERED - BOOK 2

Santi and Anna outside the Dean Road shop c. 1960

Tommy Lawson in ice-cream van c.1947

Sandy's Ice-cream Cart

Ivy Ward and Anita Alonzi with their van c. 1946. Anita drove the van and Ivy served.

FIVE

CATHERINE STREET AND SURROUNDING AREA

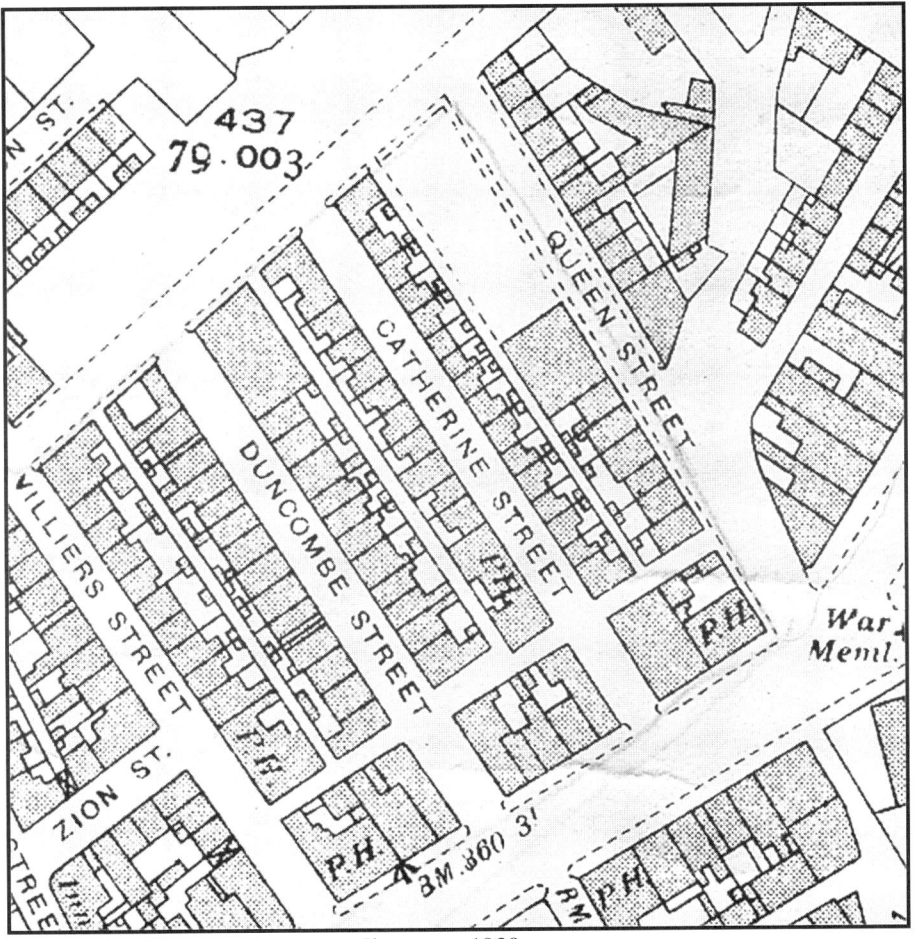

Catherine Street and surrounding area 1939.

SPENNYMOOR REMEMBERED – BOOK 2

Shortly before the Second World War and shortly afterwards the streets at the back of the High Street in the Catherine Street area were some of the most dilapidated and run down properties in the town. The local council had been thwarted in their ambition to demolish these properties and re- house their inhabitants due to the war and the severe economic conditions after it. Spennymoor had always been short of housing stock right from its beginnings, there were never sufficient houses to accommodate the newly married or single persons. Consequently quite a few of the properties were overcrowded and unhygienic to the point of being classed as slum dwellings in some cases.

The difficulty of obtaining suitable accommodation before the war is clearly apparent from Mrs. Birchall's experiences below.

" After we were married in 1936 we went to live with my Ma and Da in Ferryhill. It was all right for a while but Tommy wanted to be back in Spennymoor. There were no houses available to rent anywhere so we took rooms in Duncombe Street with Chocolate (Harry) Morgan and his wife. We had the backroom downstairs and the back bedroom upstairs, it was a two- up and two- down house. We shared the kitchen and the outside midden, an arrangement that wasn't very convenient. When they wanted to use the kitchen or the toilet the Morgans had to come through our living room. The arrangement wasn't satisfactory but it was the best we could do for ourselves at the time. We paid 5 shillings (25p.) a week rent for the rooms.

The house was in a very poor state of repair, the backyard wall was falling down and the room we were in was infested with blackclocks. We got some special powder from the council to sprinkle round the skirting boards to control the blackclocks, without much success. In all the house wasn't very clean or comfortable and any improvements we tried to make had very little effect.

We hadn't been in the house very long when my Da came down to see me, he didn't say very much or stay very long, the next thing I knew was when my Ma was at the door saying that she had found us better rooms in Barnfield Road. My Da had gone straight home and said that if anywhere better couldn't be found I would have to go back home to live. My Ma was in the Labour Party and had contacts in the town and was able to get us fixed up. The high point of living in Duncombe Street was the fact that the fish shop was only a few doors along and you could get a 1d. fish and a hap'orth of chips.

The rooms in Barnfield Road were shared as well which restricted our privacy. The other occupants were an old man and his son. The house had once been the pay office for the Weardale Works. The house wasn't actually in Barnfield Road but in what is now Derwent Terrace. We worked hard to get the rooms clean, we redecorated and it was soon how we wanted it. The old man eventually died and the son moved away and the other rooms were taken by a man and his wife. Eventually they moved into a house in Bessemer terrace and we applied to take over the whole house. The rent collector said it would be difficult because they obviously got more rent with two occupiers. However in the end we got the whole house mainly because they had seen how well we had improved our part of the house. The rent for the whole house was 12 shillings and sixpence a week. (62p.). We lived in this house until 1960 when we moved to a flat in the factory houses."

SPENNYMOOR REMEMBERED – BOOK 2

Edna Birchall.

In 1946 Thomas Sharp a planning consultant enraged the general populace of the town by describing the town as "practically slum from end to end." This remark was made all the more hurtful in that it was made in an address given to town-planners from all over Great Britain and Europe as well as being widely reported in the national press. It was denied on all counts from all sections of the community and not withstanding Mr Sharps remarks Spennymoor Councils housing programme got under way apace. Under the scheme virtually the whole of the Catherine Street area was earmarked for demolition, which eventually took place in the late1950's and early 1960's.

HOUSING

A comparatively new waiting list for houses has been compiled on a points system, and over one thousand applicants have been listed.

BUILDING PROGRAMME ALREADY EXECUTED

Estate.	"A"	"B"
Middlestone Moor Estate	8	44
Brewery Field & Derwent Terrace	—	116
Racecourse Estate	66	106
Archers Field Estate	66	—
Totals	140	266

FUTURE BUILDING PROGRAMME

Estate.	"A"	"B"
Park Estate	188	112
George Street Development Estate	108	—
York Hill Estate	128	—
Tudhoe Moor Estate	168	—
Kirk Merrington Estate	50	—
Middlestone Moor Estate	72	—
Totals	714	112

Out of the 300 houses on the Park Estate 200 are nearing completion.

"A" Houses built by Council.
"B" Built by N.E. Housing Association.

Spennymoor Housing Programme 1947.

Note the waiting list of over a thousand applicants for a council house. My wife and I joined this same waiting list in the early 1960's and although it was not as big as this we did not get a council owned property until Bessemer Park was built in 1967.

Despite the area being run down and decrepit it had a character and community spirit all of its own. Most people remember the area and its residents with a great deal of affection. As for myself I have a great deal of affection for Catherine Street as I spent a good deal of my time there when I was very young as my grandparents and great grandparents lived in the street.

SPENNYMOOR REMEMBERED – BOOK 2

Some of my first memories of Spennymoor are of Catherine Street and the surrounding area. My maternal grandparents Abraham "Abe" and May Showler, and my maternal great grandparents, Jim and Lizzy Birchall, my great aunt Suzy and her family all lived in Catherine Street. As a result of this, from a very early age, I spent a great deal of time there. Although there were some brick built houses in the street most of the houses were built of dull yellow limestone that had become progressively grimy as the years had gone on. The streets in this area had been built during the late 1850's and 1860's, among some of the first to be built in the town. They were built quickly and cheaply to accommodate pitmen and ironworkers and had changed very little from their original state over their eighty or so years of their existence. The streets were unmade compared with modern standards, as I remember they were constructed of crushed stone which provided a very uneven surface but slightly curved to allow the water to run off into the gutters in wet weather. The footpaths were paved but were very uneven and in places the road surface had broken up to form potholes. My Dad, who drove a bakers van, always drove extra carefully along Catherine Street when he came to pick us up.

The houses were generally of the same basic design, which was "two up and two down", and the amenities within were no more than primitive when compared with modern houses. The house that I spent most of my time at was that of my great grandparent's Lizzy and Jim Birchall or "Mud" and "Pad" as everyone called them. Apparently they were called this because when their children were young they couldn't get their tongues around mother and father and called them mudder and padder and the abbreviated version of these names stuck.

The house that they lived in was number 27. When you opened the front door the stairs were straight in front of you and to the left a doorway took you into the living room, which was the main room of the house. There always seemed to be someone in this room. Mud was popular with the neighbours and consequently there was a steady trickle of people popping in and out for a gossip throughout the day, added to this were the normal comings and goings of the family. The house was lit by gas, something of a great wonder to me as I came from a house lit by electricity. I never ceased to be amazed by the almost imperceptible hiss of the gas, the bright glow of the white clay covered mantle and the soft light that it gave. I could never figure out why the flame didn't travel back along the pipe and blow the gasometer up. I can remember that one of the messages I used to run was for a new gas mantle at Defty's, the hardware shop in the High Street.

The centrepiece of the front room was the enormous cast iron range, which provided heating, hot water and cooking facilities. Summer or winter I can never remember the fire not being lit, except when the chimney was being swept or the range was being black-leaded. The fireplace within the range was huge with a shelf behind the firegrate, which could be piled up with coal ready to pull down when the fire went low. Coal was in plentiful supply as the pitmen got it free and even if there wasn't a pitman in the house you could buy a load of coal cheaply or more likely than not barter for it. My great aunt Edna told me that she got her fine feather mattress for two loads of coal. There was a kettle or a pan stand on a pivot that could be swung over the fire and on that stand was the biggest cast iron kettle that I had ever seen. It used to hiss and bubble, the lid rising and falling playing little tunes to itself all day. There was a hot water boiler at the left-hand side of the range, this was filled by hand and when hot water was required the damper was opened allowing the heat of the fire to get to the boiler. The hot water was ladled from the boiler with a "laden tin" which was a tin jug with a handle this was a dangerous operation at the best of times. Sometimes food was cooked over the fire in a big cast iron pan. I can remember mussels being boiled and broth being simmered on the fire. Mud used to get a pail of mussels and they were still alive when they were dropped into the boiling water, Aunt Suzy used to have me listening for them screaming as they were tipped in. They were delicious after they had been cooked, cleaned and soused in vinegar. The broth used to be delicious, the stock being made from bacon bones or better still from boiling a ham shank. After being cooked you sucked the meat off the bacon bones but when a ham shank was cooked it meant ham sandwiches as well as broth. While the stock was being mad split peas were wrapped in a "pudden clout" and boiled up with the ham shank to make peas pudding, another delicacy, that could be added to your ham sandwich. Although I cannot remember I have no doubt that bread and teacakes were sometimes baked but the best thing that came out of the oven for me was the rabbit pies. I can close my eyes and visualise those steaming delicacies the delicious smell clinging to my nostrils yet. Another essential piece of equipment was the toasting fork, which was always hung by the side of the fire, being at hand for toasting slices of bread or pikelets, you had to make sure the fire was burning red or you got smoked toast. Above the range was the mantle shelf with a brass rod slung underneath for drying towels. Pad used to keep his pipes and baccy on this shelf along with letters and other things that had to be kept out of the prying hands and eyes of inquisitive children. Surrounding the front of the hearth was a large brass fender, the fender marked the limits as to how close you got to the fire, on cold days you stood in front of the fender and toasted your bum in front of a roaring fire. When I stayed at Mud's, Friday night was bath night, the tin bath was brought in from the yard, placed in front of the fire and filled with steaming hot water into which I was reluctantly enticed to be soaped, scrubbed and the pummelled breathless in a towel before being pyjamad and put to bed.

The living room wasn't very big but there seemed to be quite a bit of furniture packed into it. There was a table and four chairs, a dresser with draws at the bottom and a cupboard at the top, a ladder backed armchair that could be converted into a single bed, a leather chaise lounge and a rocking chair. Pride of place was taken by a large grandfather clock with a highly decorated dial on which representations of the sun moon and stars revolved with the passage of time. The main floor covering was oilcloth, which was overlaid in places by clippy mats. The clippy mats were home made, the mat frame used to be errected in front of the chaise lounge when a "clippy mat" or a "proggy mat" was being made. The mats were made from old clothing that was cut into strips. Mat making was a social occasion, everyone helped even the children, and if a neighbour called in for a cup of tea they had to earn it by sitting at the frame and "doing a bit." Close my eyes and I'm back in that room, cuddled up to Mud in the rocking chair being lulled to sleep by the sonorous ticking of the grandfather clock and the murmur of the tuneless little songs that Mud used to make up as we rocked together in front of the glowing afternoon fire.

The back of the house was divided into two, the largest part being the back kitchen which, was a very primitive affair. There was a cold water tap on the wall with a bucket underneath to catch the drips and there was a big slab sink with a draining board, which was placed beneath a small four paned window. A small table was placed by the sink with a gas ring for boiling a kettle or a pan. A gas mantle lighted the back kitchen but it always seemed dark and dingy even in broad daylight. A door on the right hand side of the back kitchen led into a walk in pantry with shelves. On one of the shelves was a meat safe with a wire gauze door to keep the flies out. On the bottom of the meat safe was a stone slab on which you placed butter, margarine, cheese, bacon or whatever you wanted to keep cool. The pots, pans, cutlery and crockery were kept in the pantry along with the food. The pantry was ventilated by a little glassless slatted window, which looked out onto the "netty" which was not more than a few feet away. This was not the best of hygienic arrangements. A door on the left-hand side of the back kitchen gave access to the backyard.

**Mud with three generations of her family outside 27 Catherine Street 1949
Suzy, her daughter against the door post, granddaughters Peggy, Dot and Bessie
And great granddaughters Pauline and Judith.**

The backyard housed the tin bath, which hung from a hook on the wall and the poss tub and the mangle. Monday was washing day and this was when the poss tub and mangle came into their own. The poss tub a galvanised metal barrel was filled with hot water, clothes and soap powder and the whole lot was agitated with a poss stick, which was manually plunged up and down to get the clothes clean. If there was any stubborn dirt it was scrubbed out by hand. The poss stick was made of a wooden shaft with a crosspiece for a handle and a copper plunger at the bottom to agitate the clothes with. When the possing was finished the clothes were then put through the mangle to get rid of the excess water. The mangle was a fearsome looking implement made of cast iron with two wooden rollers, which were turned manually with a handle. The width of the gap between the rollers could be altered so that the maximum amount of water could be squeezed out of the clothes. The narrower the gap between the rollers the more effort it took to "wring out" the clothes. After this process the clothes were possed again in clean water to rinse them and then put through the mangle again and then pegged out to dry. Washing days in those days was a demanding physical task.

The yard also had the coalhouse and the netty. The coal when it was delivered was tipped in the back street and had to be shovelled into the coalhouse through a let hole. To prevent the coals falling onto the yard when the coalhouse door was opened boards were built up to hold the coal back. The netty was a loathsome but necessary place, even to my childhood experience it was barbaric as we lived in a house in Low Spennymoor with a flushing indoor toilet. The walls were whitewashed and the wooden seat scrubbed clean and newspaper torn into squares were hung from a nail on the wall. The smell from the place was appalling even during the coolest of weather, during the warm weather it was almost unbearable. I was terrified of the netty due to the horror stories my Aunt Suzy used to tell. Across the back street was Edward's fruit warehouse, which used to attract rats in large numbers. Aunt Suzy said that some of them were as big as cats and that while you were on the netty they would jump up and bite your bum or worse. I'd seen the odd rat and had no reason to disbelieve her so I avoided the netty except in the direst of emergencies. Even then it would be in broad daylight with the door open and after I had rattled a stick down the hole to frighten off possible intruders. I never used the netty at night, I used to go into the yard and pee in the sink and even then the fear of rats overcame me and I peed in the bucket under the tap in the back kitchen. The netty was cleaned out once a week when the council workmen appeared with the horse drawn netty cart. The netty was emptied from a let hole in the back street, the contents were shovelled out into the cart and the netty was disinfected with DDT powder. Spennymor Urban District Council operated the netty carts from the depot and stables, which were next to the North Eastern Hotel. I think the council operated about five teams before being superseded by motor wagons.

**This is the type of cart used to empty netties or middens
Jack Ramshaw is the driver.**

SPENNYMOOR REMEMBERED – BOOK 2

When you went out to play you played in the street although the Park wasn't very far away. I can recall going to the park to play on the swings and the teapot lid and can also remember watching bowls matches with my Granda. Later when I was older I found my own way to the park, on route I used to stop off to play on the piles of logs and tree trunks that were dumped on waste land in Villiers Street, waiting to be turned into pegs at Burt's.

One event I remember vividly was when I was about seven or eight years old, it was during the summer in a particularly warm sunny spell of weather. Several of the mothers in Catherine Street decided to take the children down to the River Wear for a picnic. There would have been a dozen or more of us who made our way along the valley past Ox Close farm and into the woods clutching our bottles of water and sandwiches. It took a good while to reach the river but once there everyone stripped off and was soon in the water. Aunt Suzy, who was with us, warned me to beware of leaches. Leaches she said were black horrible creatures that sucked your blood. In the excitement of the moment and in my need to cool off I wasn't going to be put off by Aunt Suzy. I was straight into the water and in no time at all thoroughly enjoying myself, everything was going fine until one of the other lads gave a shriek and bolted out of the water. By the time he reached dry land and adult help he was in hysterics. He had every right to be, there hanging from his willy was one of those horrible black creatures that Aunt Suzy had warned me about. She looked at me with that little smile, never saying a word, but the look said it all, "I told you so." The leach was removed by applying a lighted cigarette to it. This event cast a shadow on the afternoon's proceedings as very few were keen to go back into the water. As for myself I haven't put a naked toe in the Wear since.

Catherine Street Families during the 1930' and 1940's
Odd Numbers.

Doggart's Department Store
1   The Connor family followed by Mr. and Mrs. Stonehouse. This was the house in the back street behind Doggart's shop.
3   Mr. and Mrs. Wilkinson and their daughter Joyce. This house had a shop front and seemed to change tenants regularly.
5   Sally Dolphin and lodger Billy Hutchinson.
7   Mr. and Mrs. Jack Thompson.
9   Mr. and Mrs. William Hirst and sons Billy and Raymond and Daughter Joyce
11 Mr. and Mrs. Topping and son Ivan.
13 Mr. and Mrs... George Littlewood and son Alf.
15 Mr. and Mrs. Mc Dermot and son Bill and daughter Pat
17 Mrs. Wood and family, John and Winny.
19 Mr. and Mrs Tommy Kelly and son Tommy.
21 Mr. and Mrs Rocks and son Jack and daughter June, followed by Mr. and Mrs Showler and son Tom and daughters Bessie, Peggy and Dorothy.
23 Mr. and Mrs. Billy O'Hara.
25 Mrs. Robinson and son Arthur and daughter Marion, followed later by Mrs. Walker and daughters Annie and Doris.
27 Mud and Pad Birchall, Mr. and Mrs. Freddy Brown and son Jim.
29 Mr. and Mrs. Watson Boyes and son Watson.
30 Mr. and Mrs. Finn and son Desmond and daughter Hazel Todd.
33 Whetherell the Printer.

SPENNYMOOR REMEMBERED – BOOK 2

Even Numbers

     Brighter Homes, painters and decorators shop.
2   Sep. Nichols the Dentist.
     Celia Kelly lived in the house behind the Dentists.
4   Albert Hotel, Mrs. Robinson and family.
6   Mr. and Mrs. Martha Sugden.
8   Mr. and Mrs. Blair.
10 Mr. and Mrs. Savage and son Bob.
12 Mr. and Mrs Hood and family followed by Mrs. Welsh and family.
14 Mrs. Mary Sugden.
16 Mr. and Mrs. Bage and family.
18 Mrs. Whitehead and son Sid.
20 Mr. and Mrs. O'Hara.
22 Mrs. Stansfield followed by Norman Cornish and wife.
24 Michael Bradley followed by Mr. and Mrs. Fitzgerald and son Tony.
26 Mrs. Tray and John Hetherington.
28 Mr. and Mrs. Hughes and sons Tommy and Bert and Daughter Beaty, followed Later by Fred Lightfoot and later still by Fred and Suzy Brown and family.
31 Mrs. Julie Cunningham.
     Round corner Mrs. Robinson and Audrey.

Catherine Street People on holiday during the 1940's
Among others: Freddy Clements, Mrs. Bainbridge, Mr. Topping, Mr. Littlewood, Mrs. Littlewood, Annie O' Hara, Mabel Stapleton, Jimmy O'Hara, Mercy Bage, Bella O'Hara, Mrs. Bestford, Beattie Angus and Harry O'Hara.

    Trips to Blackpool were popular one lady used to make one big mat a year on a frame, when she sold it the money was her Blackpool money.

There was a wonderful community spirit in Catherine Street, doors were never locked day or night and everybody helped each other. If there was anyone having a baby there was usually help from the neighbours before the midwife arrived. Similarly there was help and sympathy at hand if anyone died.

They were hard times during the twenties and thirties, people shared things and helped each other out. As far as food was concerned when all else failed we would go to the Salvation Army soup kitchen at the end of Dundas Street.

I went to the Diceys School. The headmaster was Mr. Appleby, he was over six-foot tall and as broad as a gate, there was no messing about with him, he kept strict discipline, any trouble and you were marched into his office and caned.

As children we made our own entertainment, usually playing street games such as kick the cog, tiggy and hide and seek. During the dark nights we used to play knocky nine doors, also we used to tie a button onto some thread and pin it to the middle of a window frame then tie a thread to the button and sit round the corner pulling the thread to make the button tap on the window. We made boolers (hoops) from the hoops of butter barrels, we also used these hoops at Christmas when we decorated them with berry holly mistletoe and tinsel.

There was a fish shop that we used to go to in Duncombe Street opposite to Samples the butcher. Next door was a cobbler and further along the street was an old lady who made and sold ginger beer. I used to run messages to Trotters shop in Villiers Street and Bailey's shop next to the Victoria pub in George Street. Alf Hammond had a chipvan outside the Waterloo pub and George Kirtley had a chipvan that was taken over by Berrimans. Old Mr. Berriman had a yard and stables behind Trotter's shop where he used to keep the chipvan and a hearse. He used to hire the hearse out to local undertakers and I used to go to the stables and polish the horse's hooves with oil before they went out with the hearse.

Fred Blair

Fred Blair and his mother Margaret 1936 outside their house in Catherine Street.

SPENNYMOOR REMEMBERED – BOOK 2

I was born in Catherine Street in 1931 and lived there until I was married in 1955. I slept in the back bedroom overlooking Edward's Square and can remember looking out of the window on Saturday nights and watching the fights that took place after the pubs had turned out. I can remember the travelling folk living in their vans on the square. The council had built four middens for them to use against Edward's warehouse, we used to climb on the roofs of them. We used the square which was a big open space to play on we played pop alleys mostly but also played hide and seek, tiggy and kick the cog. I also got many a clip round the ear for playing knocky nine doors during the dark nights. In 1938 the last caravan was burned on the square, the caravan had belonged to a old man who had died and according to tradition his relatives burned the van. Shortly after this Culines, the show people, took over the Square for the duration of the Second World War.

In the early days of the war I can remember going to watch a troop train leaving from Spennymoor Station. It was a long train stretching way beyond the station platform. People climbed up the steep railway embankment at the end of Bishops Close Street to wave them off as there were a lot of local TA men on the train. There were hundreds of people lined up along the embankment to see the train off.

When the new fire station was being built in Queen Street during the fifties the workmen blocked the back street behind Catherine Street so that the cart couldn't get along
 I had to empty the contents of our midden into an old bathtub and drag it along the back street to where the council cart could get access to it.

Alf Littlewood

Three Boy Scouts outside Wetherell's the Printers.
Left to right, Jackie Hamilton, Dennis Finn, Jim O'Hara

SPENNYMOOR REMEMBERED – BOOK 2

Catherine Street was a happy street, I delivered milk along there since leaving school and also lived there after I was married, I married a Catherine Street girl Beatty Hughes. I can remember that Mrs. Hughes always had a pan of broth on the go. Everyone seemed to help everyone else, if anyone was hurt at pit everybody rallied round to help.

One day I called for the milk money at Sally Dolphins and as usual I was whistling as I went into the house. Sally put her finger to her lips and pointed to the couch where Billy Hutchinson her lodger was lying. "Billy's dying." she said, "So go quietly." I took the money and tiptoed out of the house. Nobody was more surprised than I was when, that night I saw both Sally and Billy coming out of the Albert pub arm in arm at closing time. Billy was a local character, a wit and a comedian and this was typical of the antics he got up to.

There was always plenty to do we never got bored. We went dancing at the Rink, it was possible to go dancing four times a week. There was a dancing class on Monday and regular dances were held on Wednesdays, Fridays and Saturdays. If you didn't want to dance you could go to the pictures. There were fours picture halls in the town and they changed their programmes twice a week and usually showed a different film on a Sunday. If you wanted you could watch two films in one night, as there were two performances every night.

Bobby Jewitt

Bob Jewitt and Daughter Margaret on Wetherell's corner 1951.

SPENNYMOOR REMEMBERED – BOOK 2

Mrs. O'Hara's trip to Blackpool 1949.
Among others: Mr. Littlewood, Elsie Wardle, Rose Chicken, Mrs. Roberts, Norma Lord, Mrs. Littlewood, Allie Redhead, Annie Robinson, Arthur Robinson, Mabel Stapleton, Nancy Pattison, Mercy Bage, Katy Dunn, Mrs. Mapp, Mrs. Richardson, Bella O'Hara, Meg Hughes, Fred O'Hara, Beattie Angus and Jim O'Hara.

No one had much, the middens maybe stank in summer, there was no running hot water, the cooking had to be done in a fire oven but I have nothing but happy memories of the street. We listened to the wireless, we played in the street and we made our own entertainment for the most part. I can remember sitting in the dark up a passage in Queen Street with a gang of others wrapped in our coats and taking turns to tell ghost stories and being frightened to run home in the dark afterwards. In November we had a great bonfire on Queen Street Square, but the fun used to start before that. We collected the bonfire for weeks and stored it in old sheds on the square and we guarded it against raids from the "Bishies," our rivals from Bishops Close who always built a bonfire of their own.

Sometimes when our Mam was out we used to pinch sugar, vinegar and treacle and take it along to Lizzie Anne Hughes who used to make toffee for us. I can remember Phil Brown coming round the streets with his fruit cart, he had one leg. On a Friday the store baker came and we had a cake for tea, Everybody was well off on Friday as it was payday. The doors were never locked the big key used to hang on a bit string behind the door but it was never used, Nobody had anything worth pinching anyway.

We went to the pictures on a Saturday afternoon, we got 3d. It cost 1d. to get in and the remaining 2d. was spent on sweets. We used to go to the "Tiv" to see the Clutching Hand, it was a serial and although we were terrified we always went the following week to see the next instalment.

Mary O'Hara.

SPENNYMOOR REMEMBERED – BOOK 2

Entrance to Catherine Street from the High Street c.1900.

Entrance to Catherine Street from the High Street c.1956

SIX

THE SETTLEMENT

Spennymoor Settlement came into being at the instigation of Basil Henry Pease of the British Association of residential Settlements. The Association was the organising body of the Pilgrim Trust an American organisation which provided grants for the salaries of wardens and sub-wardens of Settlements. Basil Pease thought that there might be a need for Settlements in areas of high unemployment in the North. He sent Bill Farrell, later to become the warden of the Spennymoor Settlement, to make a report on whether there was a need. On the strength of Bill Farrell's report the first Settlement house was established in King Street Spennymoor in December 1931 with Bill Farrell and his wife Betty installed as wardens. Times were hard in the early thirties, the country was in recession and unemployment was endemic in the Spennymoor area. More than a quarter of the local workforce were unemployed bringing a great deal of hardship to many Spennymoor families. Most of the unemployed were miners and the Settlement offered them the opportunity of doing something to break the monotony of their enforced inactivity.

In its first syllabus the aims of the Settlement were set out as follows:

"The Settlement seeks to encourage tolerant neighbourliness and voluntary social service and provides for its members opportunity to increase their knowledge, widen their interests, and cultivate their creative powers in a friendly atmosphere." Full adult membership was open to "all persons over 18 years of age, men and women, employed and unemployed."

There was also a junior section, which comprised the Boy Scouts Troop, the Children's Play Centre and various clubs.

Women were encouraged to join as well as men. Women were under the same stressful conditions as the men if not more so as they had the responsibility of keeping their families fed and clothed and generally making ends meet.

SPENNYMOOR REMEMBERED – BOOK 2

The first year was a very successful year with a membership of over 250 men and women and a 100 children. Play-reading, local government, singing, history, women's crafts, psychology, a debating society, a sketching club, woodwork and cobbling were the subjects offered and participated in by the members. So busy was the Settlement in these early days that it became a community centre for the local area. Right from the start the premises were inadequate for the scope of what was planned and put into practise. The warden had to make the best of a small shop, with a backroom and an outhouse the living accommodation was above the shop. This state of affairs was alleviated to some extent when the Settlement received a donation to renovate and decorate an adjoining shop to house the growing membership and increased number of activities on offer. By this time the settlement had over 600 members both adult and junior to accommodate every week. They also provided facilities and services such as a County Library Branch, a club room, a games room and a Poor man's Lawyer Service.However, they did not have a room in the set up that could accommodate half of the membership. Apart from the above activities as a result of the educational work some of the able young men and women were sent to residential colleges. The Settlement also took a hand in the formation of a Town's Nursing Association, a Poultry and Allotments scheme was undertaken and a Survey into the budgets of unemployed men and their families was carried out and published in Out of The Pit by John Newsom in 1936.

By 1938 the lack of space became so desperate that it was decided that the money should be raised for the building of a new hall. C. Elgey an architect from Durham drew up the plans for a Settlement Theatre-Hall the estimated cost of which was £1,512. An application for a grant was made to the Commissioners for Special Areas and they responded generously with a grant of £1,200 leaving the balance to be raised by the Settlement. The money was raised in due course and the work on the new extension began in 1939.

```
                    SETTLEMENT  ACTIVITIES

    Sunday     –    –    –    –          Musical Appreciation Group

    Monday     –    –    –    –    –    –    Philatelic Group

    Tuesday    –    –    –    –    –    –    Theatre Company

    Wednesday  –    –    –    –    –    Archaeology Class

    Thursday   –    –    –    –    –    –    Theatre Company
                                        Religion and Philosophy Class

    Friday     –    –    –    –    –    –    Model Aero Club

    Saturday   –    –    –    –    –    –    Art Group

       Any person interested in joining any of the above Classes is
    requested to contact the Hon. Warden or the Hon. Secretary.
    All are welcome !
```

Settlement Activities 1950's

SPENNYMOOR REMEMBERED – BOOK 2

The Settlement 1932.

This was the King Street frontage of the Settlement. The shop on the right is the original shop taken over by Bill Farrell. The shop itself was the common room and behind that was Bill Farrell's Office. Bill and his wife lived in the rooms above the shop. To the left of the shop is a small house, which was not part of the Settlement. The other shop was taken over by the Settlement, Broughs the grocers had previously occupied it but they had moved to larger premises in Cheapside. This building was to provide accommodation for the County Library Branch and the living quarters for the deputy warden Jack Maddison. Behind the buildings across the back street were two large out buildings, which were used as craft shops.

Architect's isometric drawing of theNew Theatre 1938

SPENNYMOOR REMEMBERED – BOOK 2

Bill Farrell in his office 1954.

Bill Farrell and his wife Betty were originally from Liverpool. Bill was an actor who had a keen interest in social affairs. He was a very good actor and had been at the Cambridge Festival Theatre and in the West End of London. He was the first and only warden of Spennymoor Settlement, holding the position for a period of 23 years. He left the settlement in 1954 because they had lost the grant to pay his salary. He and Betty moved to Cambridgeshire where Betty became the headmistress of a village school. When Betty retired they moved back north and lived with a friend in Ormsby Hall. Bill died in July 1971 after a long illness. The photograph above shows Bill in his well organised office in his last year as warden, the room is now used as the dining room of the Bizarre Café.

Extract from The Bicycle Against The Wall.

It all started with an old bicycle I bought for thirty bob. Otherwise I would probably have continued to take the shortest road out of Spennymoor for a few years longer. But I bought that old bicycle, and it wasn't bad for an old boneshaker, so I started making detours. One of these detours led me along King Street one day and I saw some people coming out of a building with books under their arms. I hadn't much idea of what the Settlement was, but I was book-hungry, tired of westerns and adventures, so I propped my bicycle against the wall and went in.

Well, that was about 1933, and like the Settlement I was only a youngster. It was love at first sight, and before long the handlebars of my bike spent long hours conversing with the walls and those wide windows, while I browsed among good books and good pictures, and made some good friends.

Sid Chaplin

SPENNYMOOR REMEMBERED – BOOK 2

Children's Christmas Party 1932.

Children's Play Centre, 1932-42

Every Saturday morning came the patter of little feet and the chatter of many voices as the lane became thronged with eager children. They had but one breathless question, "Is the Settlement on?" It was always "on," for this was the play centre morning and all the children came. Small ones, tall ones, babies in prams and older children pushing them. Rain, hail, snow, sleet – nothing deterred them.

The play centre began in a very primitive way, a small brick hut and no equipment other than a band of willing helpers. What then attracted these children? – opportunity, for one short hour, to express themselves freely, to play with others or to play alone, to explore and experiment, to appeal for help, and to know that help would be forthcoming.

Through watching these children play we were able to make some simple provision to maintain their interest. Toys were collected for the tinies; older girls made knitted clothing for their dolls; and the older boys improvised playthings with odd scraps of materials. Thus small groups established themselves and the Centre began to take shape. Under the guidance of Miss Newman a Handwork group did much purposeful work.

The introduction of a percussion band delighted the hearts of everyone. It was a joy to watch a ten-year-old child conduct the band. The gravity with which he assumed his leadership and the earnest response of his team was enlightenment. This work was very real for these children.

The Play Centre expanded and when war came "evacuation" brought us the services of Miss Crave, who lent us nursery stock from Bensham. This was a great day. A real Nursery Group was established under trained guidance. Bricks, dolls, paint, clay, sand and water were all available and great was the joy of the children.

SPENNYMOOR REMEMBERED – BOOK 2

Highlight of the year was always the Christmas party. A team of voluntary workers spent every night for a week selecting and packing gifts. Toys came from a Guide Company in the south. Each child received not one toy but a sack full – all packed with thoughtfulness and understanding of the needs of the child who was to receive it. Party day was a real treat. The children literally staggered home with their sacks on their backs and contentment in their hearts.

Mina Martin.

Mina Martin was a teacher from Durham who originally came to the Settlement to start a Girl's Club and stayed to " become more of a Settlement member than a taker of classes."

Christmas Party 1932.

These are the youngest members of the Play Centre and can be seen holding their sacks of gifts, which had been presented by Santa Claus (Bill Farrell).

"The mams were there and the dads and everyone was waiting for Father Christmas to arrive. There was the noise of the sledge and the bells ringing as he came in! What I remember about it most was the silence. There was dead silence and just a terrific sense of wonderment when Father Christmas arrived."

Mina Martin.

Visit by The Prince of Wales 6th. December 1934.

The Duke of Windsor then heir to the throne visited the Settlement to see some the activities that took place. He saw a good range of the activities and was most impressed. He can be seen in the photograph with Bill and Betty Farrell on either side with Jack Maddison following behind.

Digging the Founds for the New Theatre 1939.
Brook Street can be seen in the background while in the middle ground the owner of Brook House is taking stock of the proceedings.

SPENNYMOOR REMEMBERED – BOOK 2

Building the new Theatre 1939.

The back of O'Hanlan Street and the Columba Hall shown to the left of the photograph.

Setting the Carving by Teesa Hess into the Building.

This carving can still be seen on the end of the building, the best vantage point for seeing it is from Low Grange Road. However, it is badly weathered and the figures are difficult to distinguish.

SPENNYMOOR REMEMBERED – BOOK 2

Herbert Dees (seated) and Robert Heslop.

Herbert Dees and Robert Heslop were two stalwarts of the Settlement Sketching Club that met every Saturday afternoon and became well known as "the Pitman's Academy." Apart from these two well-known local artists the Settlement provided tuition and inspiration for two of today's well-known local artists, Tom McGuiness and Norman Cornish.

Extracts from Sketching.

"Thank God it's Saturday dinner time!" I said to the old landlord whose property I had been painting all week, and as I began to put the ladders, steps, paint and brushes away, the old man said, "If aa wes thoo aad wark this afterneun an' git the job finished seein' its sich a fine day." "No fear!" said I, "We go out sketching every Saturday afternoon."

…..Wall pictures may have gone out of fashion in some quarters, but the joy of painting them certainly has not. The fellowship created by a Sketching Group, the friendly comradeship, and the discussions and the arguments of this and that school of painting, when Picasso and Henry Moore, Munnings and Minton, Van Gogh and Cezanne are glorified, criticised and often damnified, is a very real pleasure and is constructive. Members help each other with paint, brushes or paper and advice. Of course there is friendly rivalry, but we think that is a sure sign of a healthy group…..

Herbert B Dees.

Sketching Club Exhibition.

For many years the Sketching Club held an exhibition of paintings and drawings, the list of exhibits shown is for 1948 their sixteenth exhibition. The distinctive cover of the programme was designed by Mitchell Mackenzie a member of the Settlement.

Just look at the price of the paintings and drawings, it would be very nice to turn the clock back!

The Sketching Club still meets in the Settlement every week on a Monday night and as always was anyone is welcome to join.

SPENNYMOOR REMEMBERED – BOOK 2

The Drama Group.

The Drama Group has always been a mainstay of the Settlement right from the very beginning. Despite the fact that the original premises were too small to stage a play, play readings were a regular event under the auspices of Bill Farrell. In the early days productions were put on in St. Andrew's Mission Hall in Cheapside. When the new theatre came into being the Drama Group really came into its own. There has been at least one drama production a year put on by the Settlement Drama Group since 1932 a remarkable continuous achievement of 68 years. While other groups and activities have dropped by the wayside the Drama Group has kept the tradition and spirit of the original Settlement alive. Achieving this has not always been easy such as when membership dwindled to the extent that there were no male actors and they had to produce one act plays for females. In recent years it has fared better due in no small measure to the efforts of the late Jim Storey who was a real stalwart of the company. They are preparing for another production at the time of writing and are always looking for new recruits not only for acting but also for the important jobs back stage and at the front of the house.

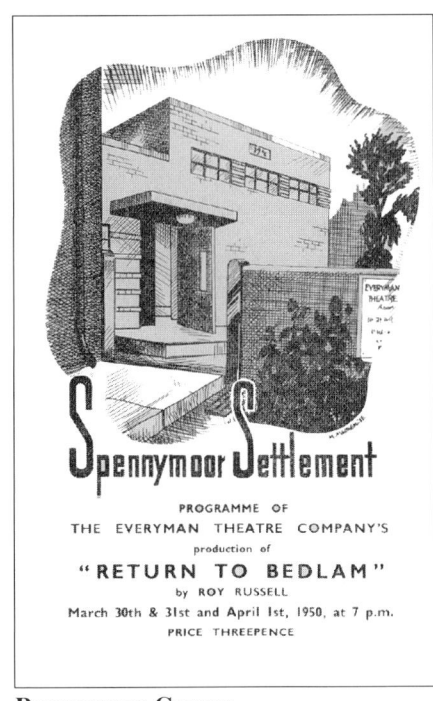

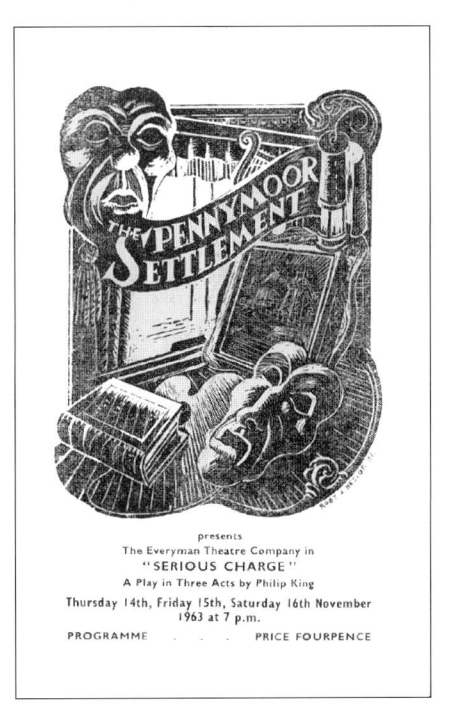

Programme Covers.
The left hand cover showing the entrance to the Theatre was designed by Mitchell McKenzie and used for a number of years it has a certain Art Deco feel about it.
The right hand cover was designed by Robert Heslop and contains a representation of everything that the Settlement stood for in its efforts to bring culture and enlightenment to miners and their families. Literature, drama, painting, music, dance they are all depicted here plus the miners lamp and pithead gear showing their pervading influence over all aspects of life in the community.

SPENNYMOOR REMEMBERED – BOOK 2

It is a lovely little theatre, we can house comfortably 120 plus. The stage is very big, in fact it is one third of the building and in the early days, it was one of the best equipped little theatres in the north of England. There was no amateur group that could boast a theatre like it. When my brother-in-law moved to Manchester and started looking around for somewhere to produce plays, he said we at the Settlement didn't know how lucky we were to have such equipment and such a theatre.

Edith Kirtley

Edith joined the Settlement in 1942 and still takes an active part in the Drama Group.

Extract from The Production Machine.

It is no accident that my most vivid recollections of the theatre are concerned with production rather than acting. It is all part of the training I received there, and a part, which I have found invaluable since, as a teacher of drama myself. I served my apprenticeship in every department – "props," promoter, assistant stage manager and assistant electrician. In the latter capacity I helped to install the stage electrical system, and learned that fitting innumerable fuses is not an honour to be sought, but a "dirty job" always delegated to the electrician's second mate.

Dorothy Martin

Dorothy Martin used to run the Girl's Club at the Settlement.

The Cast of Juno and the Paycock 1952.
Among others: Betty Farrell, Bill Farrell, Edna Spence, Fred Dunn, Fred Lightfoot, Jim Storey, Muriel Lamb, Carrie Johnson, Maureen Gash and Rita Cummings.

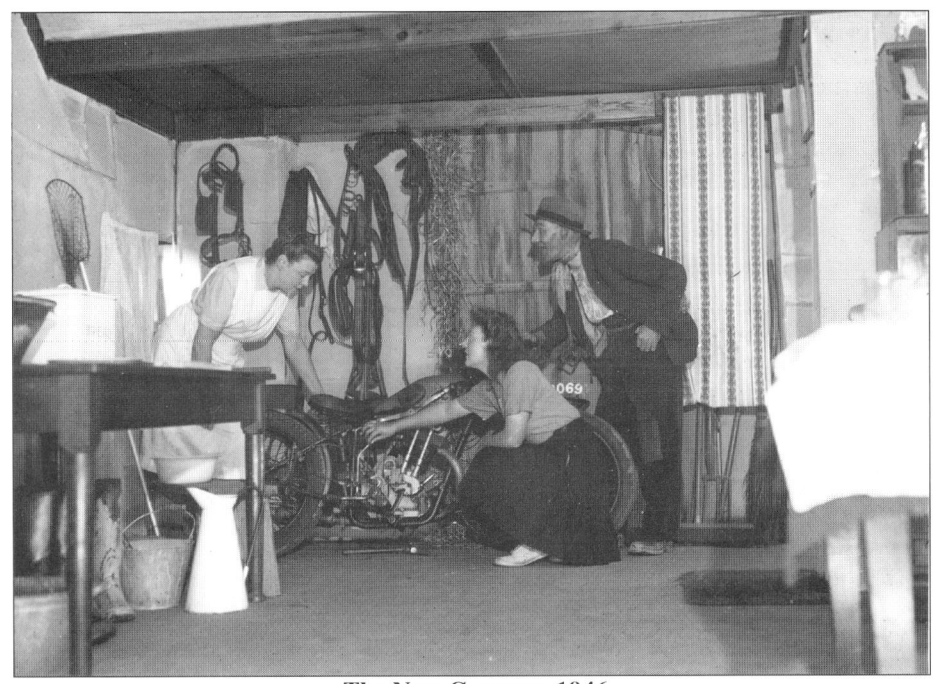

The New Gossoon 1946.
Lillian Banham, Ivy Bennett and George Rowntree.

The Piper of Ord
Sylvia Dobson, Ann Blakey, Fred Lightfoot, Jim Storey, Rena Simpson, John Robinson and Brenda Savage.

SPENNYMOOR REMEMBERED – BOOK 2

Teesa Hess.

Teesa Hess was a German sculptress who came to teach at the Settlement in 1936, she taught sculpture and art. She stayed at the Settlement until 1939 and then had to return to Germany because her father was ill. Teesa Hess became well regarded as a sculptress she entered a convent but continued to teach art and sculpture for a good number of years. She certainly left her mark on the settlement as she carved the sculpture, which still sits near the top of the theatre building (see page 122).

Extract From What Price Happiness – autobiography of Dicky Beavis.

….. "Another was a refugee from Hitler's Germany; a woman sculptor, a Jewess. At the time the Settlement was still in the throes of getting modernised and the woman wanted to carve a headstone to be placed at the top of the building; two heads bonded together, denoting worker and teacher united. Trevor Buckley who had such a rugged head was chosen as the worker, (although he made plenty of wisecracks about not really qualifying as a worker: he had been employed while in the army by the War Office - digging the dead bodies up from the First World war for reinternment – but since then he'd been unemployed and used to say "I'll have to wait for another war, before I get another job.") Well he sat, while the bits of stone were chiselled to make this monument. I don't know who sat for the woman's face, but the stone is still there all weathered away now. It depicts what the Settlement of Spennymoor stood for – Worker and Teacher, bonded together means progress."

Trevor Buckley by Teesa Hess

The two woodcarvings were done as models for the sculpture that went on top of the theatre building, the one on the right is a representation of Trevor Buckley.

(All personal reminicences are taken from the 21 Birthday booklet of the Settlement)